Digital Marketing

Advanced Strategies to Start, Acquire, Retain, and Scale a Successful Digital Marketing Agency

Richard Hedberg

Your Free Gift

As a way of saying thank you for your purchase, I'm offering the ebook, *Marketing on Click LLC: A Business Plan Example*, for FREE to my readers.

To get instant access, just go to:
https://ll-publishing.aweb.page/digital-marketing-free-bonus

Inside this ebook you will discover:

• Insider knowledge on formatting and structuring a winning business plan
• Proven strategies for what information to include and how to present it
• Secrets to using the right language and terminology to capture the attention of investors
• Exclusive insights on identifying potential gaps or weaknesses in your own plan
• The key to creating a business proposal that sets you apart from the competition
• And so much more!

Don't miss out on this opportunity to unlock the secrets of a winning business plan. Grab your free ebook today and start creating a plan that will take your business to the next level!

Introduction

A small business is an amazing way to serve and leave an impact on the world you live in.

— Nicole Snow

Marketing is something we all know a little about. We practice it all the time across every stage of our lives. Ever since the start of life itself, we humans have been practicing marketing by promoting ourselves to the greater society, building relationships, and convincing others to achieve personal goals. Even when you were back in high school looking to make new friends and impress that special someone, you were marketing yourself.

Marketing is a big part of my life, and I am very passionate about it. Aside from strategic planning, I believe the marketing component is the real deal that sustains a business and allows for a consistent flow of income. This is why one of the very first businesses I started was a digital marketing agency, because I started with what I was passionate about—and I got huge value out of it.

It was a great learning experience, and I am here to share with you how you can succeed in building a digital marketing agency just like I did—only you'll have a much easier time doing it better as you learn from my mistakes! Just like many others, I made some mistakes at the beginning, which saw me struggle for a few months to land clients, and I had to make it through those few months of dealing with high recurring costs and little money coming in.

However, as each month went by, I slowly learned what errors I had made and rectified them. One of the biggest credits goes to having a proper business plan, which I discuss in great detail in one of my books. Other than that, it's about the mindset of determination to keep learning and evolving with the market, while at the same time developing yourself. If the market is pushing you down and you do nothing about it, then you will be left hanging, and no one will give a damn. But if you do rise up and remain open to learning and adapting, then you will still be in the race.

I want to talk about this mindset first, because this book is dedicated to you. You are most likely an entrepreneur looking to start your digital marketing agency—which is, of course, a business. Having the patience, faith, and growth mindset to adapt and get through each challenge in your own way is the strength of a successful entrepreneur. So, I hope this first lesson I share will be in your heart always. Let's dive deep into the main subject.

Introduction

Forget the Past: It's Time to Look at the Present

Every business needs marketing in some form. The main reason is to find clients, but for me, it's simply about being known in the world. Marketing is about recognition. If your target client doesn't know who you are, then it doesn't matter if you have the best product or service in the world. You won't sell a thing. However, if you put yourself in front of them, then there is a high chance that you will be known to them, and you can sell them your product or service.

Many businesses are left behind nowadays because they are still learning and using old, traditional marketing concepts from the last century. They are being left in the dust by other competitors who have adapted and are implementing modern-day tactics. Traditional marketing methods, such as printing ads in newspapers, magazines, and on billboards or airing ads on television, aren't as effective as they used to be. I wouldn't say they are finished, though. They can still benefit some businesses, just not to the degree that they used to.

No one really reads newspapers or magazines these days. They don't even watch TV ads like they used to. It's all because of amazing creations like smartphones, the PC, and other digital devices; people spend a lot of time logged in on their screens consuming content wherever they can find it. The biggest benefit of these digital devices is that people get instant access to content with a few taps. That's all it takes... a few taps.

This is why marketers have now switched to marketing through digital channels like websites, emails, and social media, including Facebook, Instagram, LinkedIn, etc., as well as other digital platforms. They have a much better chance of being noticed online than they would have through the offline methods. And this intentional marketing through digital channels is what we call digital marketing.

Why Digital Marketing Will Keep Growing

Digital marketing is not only here to stay; it will continue booming. With the development of technology and many innovations coming through, businesses will have to rely on and master marketing through digital channels to ensure leads keep coming through. This is why this market is lucrative, and even someone who is a beginner and doesn't have a solid degree can easily learn the concepts of digital marketing and become an expert.

The following are a few reasons why digital marketing should be taken seriously.

Control of Reach

In marketing, reach means the size of the audience that you will expose your ads or marketing campaigns to. This is essential for a marketer so that they have a good chance of reaching interested prospects, who will then hopefully move into their marketing funnel. A marketing funnel basically denotes the journey of your potential customer from initial contact all the way to the purchasing stage. And for getting more prospects into your marketing funnel, you definitely need to expose ads to a large number of people. That's common sense.

However, digital marketing not only helps you to expose ads or marketing efforts to a large number of people; it also allows you to control the reach. If you are marketing for a local carpentry business in Dover, Delaware, and their target audience are only citizens of Dover, then you can implement local reach toward the people of Dover. On the other hand, if you are marketing for an online coaching business whose target audience can be anyone across any geographical location, then you can implement global reach and have your ads target toward many people across various countries.

Intentional Targeting

Traditional marketing, such as having posters or billboards in one location, is just hoping that one day your ideal prospect will be there in that very same location and notice your ad. But in digital marketing, you can intentionally get these ads in front of your ideal prospects through paid Facebook ads, Instagram ads, and much more, so that you don't need to wait and hope that prospects get excited by the message your ads convey. Thus, digital marketing is the more effective type of marketing.

Arsenal of Marketing Strategies

While traditional marketing has a few options marketers can rely on, digital marketing has tons of strategies you can use and many different platforms that you can use to execute your marketing strategies.

From strategies like pay-per-click (PPC) and search engine optimization (SEO) to using influencers on platforms like Facebook and LinkedIn, marketers have a digital playground where they can test their strategies and post various content in the form of blogs, podcasts, newsletters, infographics, and much more to attract their ideal prospects.

Instant Measurement and Feedback

What I love most about digital marketing is its ability to give marketers instant feedback on how their marketing campaign is functioning in real-time and provide insight on where they can improve or correct mistakes.

Analytics are available on many digital marketing interfaces, including Facebook ads and the LinkedIn campaign manager. You can study how your audience engages with your posts and measure metrics to see whether your ad is well-aligned to generate leads.

Cost-Effective Nature

When it comes to saving on costs, businesses can rely on digital marketing because these marketing tools are more cost-effective compared to printing in magazines or airing ads on television. All of this supports the point that you will waste fewer resources and, of course, money when you opt for digital marketing tools over traditional marketing methods.

Don't Hesitate to Start Your Digital Marketing Agency

I know the general feeling of procrastinating to start a business. One of the biggest reasons is the fear of being a failure or losing a lot of money you invest in your business. The other reason is the difficulty of managing a business in the long run. However, if you put those two reasons behind you and understand why starting a digital marketing agency is probably (in my opinion) the best type of business to start as a beginner, then there won't be any hesitation.

First and foremost, starting a digital marketing agency is definitely worth it because businesses *need* your services. What do businesses require to achieve their financial goals? Customers. How can they get customers? Marketing. Where can they get effective marketing services from? You. Whether you are providing marketing services for product-based businesses or service-based businesses, they need a continuous flow of leads coming in, and they will rely on you to make that possible—especially service-based businesses, since services are perishable by nature.

Since more and more businesses are in need of your digital marketing services, this makes starting an agency a profitable business, as it creates a consistent income stream. The income potential is high. You could be offering digital marketing services for a local bakery that sells products at $20, or you could be marketing for a software company that sells their products for more than $1,000. The latter provides you with more income earning potential.

Your income is going to be sustainable, because this is what I learned when I offered digital marketing services to businesses: When a client is happy about you bringing in leads for their business and helping them make money, they will undoubtedly keep you. Now, you already have one long-term client that is your sustainable income source, so imagine how your agency will continue to attract and impress more long-term clients. The sky's the limit.

This is why it is a safe business, and you can easily scale your business from offering digital marketing services by yourself to hiring a large virtual team that you can delegate duties to. This is the new way of doing business and making better profit margins; not the old days when you invested loads into setting up a shop only to have to shut it down because you couldn't attract enough customers.

Moreover, you are creating jobs for others when you start a digital marketing agency. Especially if you are doing this virtually and reaching out to many clients, you will need a lot of people on your team with the right skills to assist you. Therefore, you are also doing a good deed by creating jobs for others.

How This Book Can Help You

This book is for anyone who is interested in this topic. You could be someone who is going to start a digital marketing agency, or perhaps you're already running one and are seeking to learn how to make your business run more smoothly.

Whatever the case, this book is organized to address your worries when it comes to starting and managing a profitable digital marketing agency, landing clients, delivering results by adding value for those clients, and retaining them for the long-term.

I will share with you in this book my knowledge and the model to run an effective digital marketing agency by using real-life examples. As a result, you will be confident enough to run your own successful digital marketing agency in no time. Let's get started, and I wish you an enjoyable and informative read!

Chapter 1

Digital Marketing—Know the Concepts

Ignoring online marketing is like opening a business but not telling anyone.

— KB Marketing Agency

In this first chapter, we will go through the basic marketing concepts you need to know about and how you can associate them with digital marketing. This is important even if you decide on a hands-off approach that lets your agency run independently. Having basic marketing knowledge is essential for making important decisions and providing effective services to your clients.

The Traditional Marketing Mix

The marketing mix is one of the most established marketing strategies and is useful for many businesses as they conduct their marketing. The early establishment of the marketing mix consists of the four major Ps. These Ps are as follows: Product, Price, Place, and Promotion. Here is a breakdown of each of these four Ps in depth.

Product

As the name suggests, this is the product you are selling. The product can be tangible or intangible in nature. That is why you can include both products and services under this component. In digital marketing terms, this denotes the products or services your agency offers to the client. This may be services such as website building, paid advertising, social media marketing, etc.

Besides determining your product, it is also where you look to develop the lifetime value of your product/services by doing more research, analyzing your competitors, releasing innovative features, and ensuring it is up-to-date with the market. For instance, your paid advertising service might be a top-notch service for your clients for the first few years, especially when you leverage social media platforms like Facebook and LinkedIn. However, things can change. Your competitors continue to grow, and there is a rise of a new social media platform from out of the blue where businesses now target their paid ads.

In this situation, you would want to adapt your services and learn to implement paid ads on the new social media platform, or else improve the features of your current service. This way, you won't get left behind and will be able to maintain and gain clients over the course of this shift. The product component of the marketing mix plays a huge role in how your marketing runs successfully throughout each year.

Price

This component of the marketing mix indicates the price you will set for your product/service. This is where your pricing strategy can be key. For instance, if you are a new digital marketing agency just entering the market and looking to build your first few initial clients, then you will need to cut down your prices below market value. This is known as penetration pricing, and it is common for new entrants to adopt this pricing strategy to combat the big established agencies and ramp up their first few clients.

Later on, when your agency builds a solid client base, you can adjust your prices to meet market value, and when there is more demand for your services, you can offer them at a premium. Value-based pricing is a good pricing strategy as it helps you to understand how to price your digital marketing services based on the clients' perceived value of the service. This can be determined by analyzing the clients' preferred budget they would spend on specific digital marketing services through online surveys, interviews, and so on.

Place

Place in the marketing mix basically refers to where you will distribute your product/services to your ideal target market. Moreover, this can also help your clients understand where to find and learn about your services. For instance, your digital marketing agency could be based in North America. It would make more sense to target your marketing activities to the people of North America by using common social media tools such as Facebook, Instagram, and LinkedIn than, let's say, in China where you will find the people don't use Facebook and have their own social media platform.

However, many digital marketing agencies these days do offer services to several geographical locations, so this could depend on your business objectives and who your ideal target market is. But this component of the marketing mix is all about determining your distribution channels and where you will find your ideal clients.

Promotion

The fourth P involves the different promotional methods used to advertise and promote your product/service through these marketing channels. This is basically "how" you are going to make them reach your ideal market. For example, you can find digital marketing clients on a platform like LinkedIn, but you'll need somewhere to start.

This is where you should use marketing promotional tools such as publishing content, LinkedIn sponsored ads, InMails (private messaging in LinkedIn), and Sales Navigator (sales tool to filter and find ideal prospects). This is your collection of marketing tools that you can use to find prospects on each platform and help them learn more about your services.

The four Ps of the marketing mix serve mainly product-based businesses. However, as the service industry kept booming, three additional Ps added to the mix that tailor toward the service-based businesses. They are People, Process, and Physical evidence.

Let's break down these three Ps.

People

This basically refers to the people who interact with your clients throughout the marketing and sales process—all the way from initial contact to the purchasing stage. When you relate this to a digital marketing agency, this may be the people you have on your marketing and sales teams who work hard to land clients.

Process

Process is the idea and framework behind how you will look to execute your services for your ideal clients in the best possible manner. This is a crucial element, especially for service-based businesses, and it requires intricate planning and lots of trial and error to determine the best service model for clients. When you relate it to a digital marketing agency, this might be how you manage an ad campaign for your client from the moment they sign a contract with you to the moment you fulfill your duties or deliverables as promised and ensure client satisfaction.

Physical Evidence

This denotes all the tangible things and experiences that clients can experience and provide feedback on. In digital marketing terms, this can be confirmation emails you send to your client when they sign a contract with you, or it can be the metrics or analytics you show to them that measures the progress of the marketing campaigns going well for their business.

Eventually, you find seven Ps in the marketing mix and this can be useful when you start a digital marketing agency so that you address each of these components and not miss out on delivering the ultimate client satisfaction.

Digital Marketing Concepts

Since digital marketing involves a lot of interactions with your customers in the digital world, you will need to understand some more marketing concepts that can help you develop a solid framework when you start your agency.

Outbound vs Inbound Marketing

For marketers, it is important to understand the difference between outbound and inbound marketing. This is something I prioritize based on my agency's time management capabilities and availability of resources. Outbound marketing, otherwise known as push marketing, is you going out there and directly looking to engage and contact interested prospects and clients. Some examples of outbound marketing include emails, messaging, and phone calls. This leans toward the sales spectrum, and you are expecting to get results quickly in the form of leads.

On the other hand, inbound marketing, or pull marketing, is making the customers come to you and contact you first. Some examples of inbound marketing include publishing content in the form of blog posts, videos, or podcasts. Or it might involve your website design—its presentation and portfolio of clients impresses visiting prospects and convinces them to reach out to you first. This leans toward the holy grail of what marketing should be and relies on a long-term commitment. It also requires patience from marketers to start seeing results quickly.

Coming back to how I use these two strategies to my advantage, during the initial stages of my agency, I had to aggressively implement outbound marketing strategies, since we were basically an unknown entity in the marketplace without prior clients and we needed to learn more about our clients in general. After we established ourselves in the marketplace and improved our brand positioning, we constantly were able to receive leads without trying because we implemented inbound marketing strategies, and this made it easier for us to save money for our marketing/sales team and focus on other important aspects of the business. As you can see, it can be situational, but having a blend of both outbound and inbound marketing for your agency can do wonders.

Digital Brand Positioning

When you start a digital marketing agency, you must look to prioritize providing unique value to your clients so that they will remember you. This is where thinking as a brand helps. And that is why you should pay attention to your brand positioning in the digital world.

It is much easier to establish a reputable brand image online nowadays than it was in the past when there was no internet. You can establish a brand presence by promoting your business online frequently and showing your market how you are unique compared to your competitors.

This can be established by sharing your authentic brand story, publishing creative content via videos, blog posts, infographics, etc., using specific color themes that resonate with your agency, and engaging with prospects and the online community with the purpose to serve them.

Targeting

As a digital marketer or entrepreneur, targeting your ideal clients involves a lot of planning. You can't reach out to just anyone because not everyone will require your services. Hence, it is important to determine the specific set of customers that will be interested in your services.

For instance, if your agency offers social media marketing as your primary service, reaching out to influencers online and helping them promote their content would be the right form of targeting. In addition to that, you must also look to protect your clients' privacy and keep information confidential so that you won't be entangled in any lawsuits.

Platforms

For digital marketing agencies, you will need to make use of different platforms to land clients and also conduct business with them. These platforms can be best differentiated for your understanding as follows:

- Advertising platforms: LinkedIn, Google, Instagram, and Facebook
- Analytics platforms: Google Analytics to measure performance metrics
- Email marketing platforms: Mailchimp to send newsletters and get subscribers
- Social media platforms: Facebook, and LinkedIn to connect with an audience and manage social media accounts
- Content management platforms: help to create, manage, and publish content
- Customer relationship management platforms: Salesforce to help store customer details and track interactions throughout the typical sales process

Skills of the Trade

For your digital marketing agency, it is essential to keep learning and incorporating the various skills that are beneficial in the market. There are a lot of competitors out there, and the skills you and your agency possess will help you stand out from the crowd. This means knowing and using different media tools like video, graphic design, and editing audio podcasts.

Other essential skills include presentation and engagement. These are skills like speaking and participating online, producing insightful content, communicating to engage with clients online and understand their needs, project management for managing many digital marketing projects, and analytical skills such as understanding data and being able to present insightful reports that are beneficial to the agency's growth and planning.

Content

As a digital marketer, everything is centered around content because content helps you to deliver a specific message to your ideal target market. Creating up-to-date and quality content for your audience can help build relationships and reflect a positive brand image. The idea is to give value by producing content and not expect anything in return from your audience.

Digital Analytics

In digital marketing, analytics is essential, and this can be your savior. There are many digital analytics tools out there, but the common ones like Google Analytics to measure website metrics and Google Trends to research online search trends can come in handy at the start.

Processes

Next up, for any digital marketing agency to succeed, your processes need to run smoothly, often with several working at once. This involves processes such as crafting/submitting proposals to clients, managing different projects, communicating needs and progress to different stakeholders, and various administrative tasks behind each department.

An organizational hierarchy helps to establish order, with every employee having defined roles, such as digital marketing director, manager, coordinator, assistant, executive, etc., with respective responsibilities and duties.

Media Mix: The Modern-Day Marketing Strategy

Another important concept that is essential to understand when pursuing your digital marketing journey is the media mix. It is fundamentally a combination of media channels your business will use to attain your marketing goals.

For instance, a media mix strategy I used for one of my clients—a cosmetics company—was a blend of both online and offline marketing channels. The aim of the ad campaign was to promote a new eyeliner that makes women's eyes stand out with beauty and elegance.

Our agency made use of offline channels such as billboards in a couple of key cities. When it came to online channels, the company website's homepage was the main hub to promote the new exotic product. This encouraged interested buyers to click on the homepage image, which led them directly to the landing page to get offers and to purchase the eyeliner.

Other online channels we utilized included promoting the content in video form on the company's YouTube channel and then utilizing paid ads on Facebook and Instagram. As you can see, the mix of these marketing channels to identify and leverage the best chance for conversions helped us meet our marketing goals.

Using Your Media Mix to Maximize Marketing Effectiveness

Going in-depth about the media mix, another concept that allows businesses to understand how their marketing messages are landing with their target customers is known as media mix optimization. Businesses make use of this process to reveal the combination of marketing channels that is most effective.

My agency makes use of this process every time when conducting a media mix strategy so that we can invest our time and resources into leveraging the right combination of channels for our clients and also to optimize our marketing strategy. It is important to note that this method is more useful when analyzing online marketing channels because you have access to data analytics to determine the ROI of these marketing campaigns. However, when analyzing offline methods like billboards, posters, etc., it isn't worth considering.

As you can see, media mix optimization is the process of getting to understand these things. But to go in-depth and understand the "how" of it all, this is where media mix modeling comes into play. Otherwise known as marketing mix modeling, this is a technique that helps businesses to analyze the marketing campaign's impact and to study broadly each channel's conversion rates.

For instance, I'll share how this was useful for my agency during our early days of the startup. One of our clients—an ecommerce skincare company—was looking to promote their new style of eco-friendly packaging to have their products conveniently delivered to female customers. We implemented a marketing mix using online channels such as social media platforms (specifically Instagram, Facebook, and Pinterest), their promotional company website homepage, and also email newsletters. We set the landing page as the place to get conversions and also to track where prospects were coming from.

We found that there were more inquiries and conversions through social media channels—especially Pinterest in particular (since there is a large female audience on that platform). On the other hand, there were fewer site interactions and visits with the company website homepage, and this led to fewer conversions. This allowed us to leverage the use of social media platforms (Pinterest in particular) and invest more of our resources to deliver results for our client.

Moreover, this helped us to spend less of each client's budget on the company website page as well as email newsletters, which didn't bring in significant results. This was a crucial decision, as the client's budget was limited and we needed to churn out results on a tight deadline. Thanks to the process of media mix optimization and modeling, we were able to quickly identify and use the right marketing channels for our clients.

If you do implement the media mix in your digital marketing strategy and want to optimize it for better results, I would recommend you consider collecting more personal level data to begin with. The clarity of the data and how much this data tells you about each visitor and prospect can help you.

For instance, metrics such as visits to your landing page can be shallow and are basically just numbers. But if you are able to track back to where visitors came from, identify which social media platform they use, and get a bit more information about their background, this helps you to narrow down the pool to a group of interested prospects who display similar demographics.

Another thing you should pay attention to is the way you report the data. Measuring data from an offline ad, such as on billboards, and reporting this can be quite difficult compared to online campaigns. You may need to deploy extra manpower to measure these things or find other creative ways to do so. In most cases, removing these offline ad campaigns and leveraging online ones instead helps most businesses today.

Also, one useful indicator you can use is to note how your brand is being talked about in social media. You will find people tagging your brand, so you can glean the positives and negatives based on their feedback. You can use this as a kind of free survey and gain a lot of insight that will help you shake up your media mix strategy. We know that public opinion matters for how you shape your marketing strategies.

Understanding Customer Lifetime Value

We will end this chapter by discussing one concept that is very important to your business: customers. Depending on the type of business you are running and the industry you are in, you will have several choices to make regarding how you want to achieve your goals.

If your target for the first year is to make $500,000, you can attain this in a few ways. You could sell your services for $1,000 per customer. This means you'd need 500 customers to earn $500,000 in the first year. Or, you could sell your services for $500,000 to only one customer.

Does that sound crazy? And I'm not talking about high-ticket selling, either (selling expensive products/services that are of high value). I'm saying one customer could bring you an accumulated revenue of $500,000 over a period of time, depending on how well you provide quality service to the customer. In this way, you would be able to retain them so they will want to only work with you in the future.

Moreover, this depends on how successful their business becomes and whether they are able to provide enough funding to work with you, because as a digital marketer, your job is to help them make money through your marketing efforts. In digital marketing, repeat businesses are common, and your agency should play a vital role in establishing long-term relationships with your customers to create a sustainable and profitable revenue stream from each client.

The total revenue that a customer brings you over the entire lifetime relationship with your business is known as Customer Lifetime Value, or CLV in short. It is basically the financial value of your individual clients. So, this means even if you prioritize your marketing funnel (a funnel describes your customer's journey with you), you need to understand that CLV is just as important.

Importance of CLV

Knowing the CLV of each customer can help your business in many ways. It is a metric that helps you learn how you can provide better service to your customer, understand the quality and competitiveness of your pricing, and get a clear picture of the products/services you sell best. CLV helps you to understand your marketing strategy's impact by showing from which source and demographics you are winning loyal customers.

This information will help you to better align your marketing efforts and leverage those overlooked areas, for example. As a result, it improves the clarity of your decision-making for your marketing strategies as well as your return on investments when you look to set short-term and long-term goals.

Regardless of the benefits CLV can provide your business, it is the effective customer relationship that you build with each of your clients that is going to matter most. Every customer wants a pleasant experience while their needs are fulfilled, and this is where you can help to achieve that.

In a nutshell, CLV helps to narrow down demographics, analyze each customer's loyalty and the effectiveness of your marketing efforts, lead to better decision-making, and, of course, achieve better profits in the long run.

How to Calculate CLV

Theoretically, you now understand the meaning of CLV. But now, let's look at how you can calculate this so you can put the theory into practical use, like I do with my business. For that, you need to follow a step-by-step calculation process.

Step 1: Average Order Value

Firstly, you need to calculate the average order value, and this can be found by dividing your total revenue (income earned) over a specific period by the number of orders or sales during that period.

For example, let's say for the first six months of your business, you generated around $30,000 in revenue. This revenue came from 100 orders. So, your average order value will be $300 (30,000/100).

Step 2: Average Purchase Frequency

The next thing to calculate will be the average purchase frequency. This denotes the average number of orders or sales you get from unique customers. So, if you have a customer who placed more than one order during that period, they should still be counted once when you calculate.

Let's take our previous example. Your business generated around $30,000 from 100 orders/sales, but they come from 25 customers. Here, your average purchase frequency will be 4 (100/25).

Step 3: Average Customer Lifespan

The next step is to determine the time period of each customer relationship right up to the day the relationship dissolves. This can be easier to calculate on a long-term basis if your business is established with a larger client base.

For smaller and newer businesses, the sample size can be less, so it is better to find this by calculating the "Churn" rate:

Churn rate = (Customers at the beginning of a specific period - Customers at the end of the period)/ Customers at the beginning of the period

The formula for calculating the average customer lifespan is:

Customer Lifespan = 1/Churn Rate

For example, let's say you have 9 customers at the beginning of a month but around 8 customers at the end of that same month. Your churn rate will be 0.11 ([9-8]/9), and your average customer lifespan is 9 months (1/0.11).

Step 4: Customer Lifetime Value

Using the first three steps, you can calculate your CLV with this formula:

CLV = Average Order Value (Step 1) x Average Purchase Frequency (Step 2) x Average Customer Lifespan (Step 3)

So, taking the values of our example, the CLV will be = $300 x 4 x 9 = **$10,800**

This means you have accumulated or can expect around $10,800 from each customer over the lifetime of your business relationship with them.

This chapter has helped you to understand the digital marketing concepts and the importance of how each customer can impact your business growth. The next chapter will take you through defining important goals that can determine your business's growth and success.

Key Takeaways From This Chapter

- The traditional marketing mix consists of seven Ps—Product, Price, Place, Promotion, People, Process, and Physical Evidence.
- Some of the important digital marketing concepts involve balancing your inbound and outbound marketing, positioning your digital brand, implementing effective targeting, leveraging digital platforms, incorporating skills that provide value to customers, producing content, and utilizing digital analytics and processes that shape your business.
- A media mix is a combination of media channels that your business uses to achieve marketing goals. You can use media mix optimization and modeling to understand which marketing channels provide better returns on investment and generate profitable leads and conversions from those channels.

- Customer lifetime value is the total revenue that a unique customer provides you during their lifetime relationship with your business.
- To calculate CLV, multiply your average order value with the average purchase frequency and average customer lifespan.

Chapter 2

Measure Digital Marketing Goals

*Without goals, and plans to reach them, you are like a ship
that has set sail with no destination.*

— Fitzhugh Dodson

This next chapter is all about determining your
digital marketing goals and measuring them. This
is an important step in your journey as a digital
marketing entrepreneur, as measuring goals helps to analyze
your progress in each phase of your business and also to optimize growth. When you start a business, making money is
definitely the first objective that comes to mind—but let's
change that. You should think about growth!

Building a business is all about expansion and building an
empire so you don't have to constantly hustle to keep things
going. You'll also need an effective organizational structure.
Having said that, it all depends on how well you pay attention
to your business. Hence, this chapter will walk you through

the importance of setting goals and measuring them regularly in order to make improvements in the long run.

Identifying Your Digital Marketing Goals

Setting milestones for your goals is smooth once you identify them, but this isn't always so easy. This was my struggle early on, despite having lots of knowledge regarding the subject. I was lacking inspiration for what I really needed to achieve. Not knowing exactly what you're going for can be a terrible feeling, and I struggled to understand what I really needed to focus on to grow a digital marketing agency. I did identify and set some goals here and there, but I always feared that something was missing.

I felt that my goals were all over the place, and they seemed disorganized. In fact, I was confused about whether I was pursuing the right goals for my digital marketing agency or overlooking the important ones. I needed some advice, so I started searching. Then one night, after hours of browsing the internet, I stumbled upon the information that would help me in a big way, and I hope this will help you, too.

Let me introduce to you the "five S" framework that can help you identify the best goals for your digital marketing agency and also remove any fear that you might be missing some-thing as you pursue growth for your agency. The five S framework includes Sell, Speak, Serve, Save, and Sizzle. Let's break down each one of these to learn more.

Sell

The basic intention of selling is to grow sales over time. And this is what most entrepreneurs think of right off the bat when they start a business. This department deals with all the transactions to make tons of revenue and eventually, profit. Hence, setting goals such as growing your number of sales, implementing strategies to ensure a smooth workflow in the sales funnel, and creating more avenues for lead generation are some of the common goals under this component.

Speak

This component for goal-setting focuses on how close you can become with your ideal customers to engage with them effectively. Digital channels are the best places to leverage one-on-one communication with your ideal customers and understand them better. Choosing the best digital channels to communicate with prospects, producing insightful content to engage with customers, and planning meetings to talk with your audience are some goals under this component.

Serve

To serve is basically to add value for your audience or target customers. The focus here is to identify and deliver on different ways to offer the best value to your audience and increase satisfaction. Hence, surveys to get familiar with customer feedback, remodeling your service strategy, and conducting in-depth market research to learn about pain points are some examples of goals in this category.

Save

Saving money is another fundamental part of running a business, mainly to increase profit margins. Moreover, it helps you allocate your digital marketing budget correctly and focus on delivering more value to your customers. Goals such as trimming your online marketing channel spending, reducing ad expenditures, and identifying areas in the business where costs can be reduced are some examples.

Sizzle

To add some sizzle means to make your brand exciting so more people will talk about it online. This is the ultimate component of your business growth strategy, and it focuses on setting goals related to branding. Setting goals such as producing content regularly, engaging frequently with the audience online, or running innovative brand campaigns will help make your digital marketing agency sizzling hot!

Using these five components, I was able to identify my goals and organize them better. This helped massively for my agency's growth, and I'm sure it will do the same for you.

Setting Digital Marketing Goals: Being SMART

Digital marketing goals are essential for ensuring agencies stick to a plan to generate more leads, improve their conversion rates, boost their sales funnel, and build a good brand presence online. However, setting the parameters for them can be just as crucial as identifying them. Early on, I made some mistakes, and one of them was setting vague goals.

One that immediately springs to mind is "increase sales." I set this goal early on in the initial months of startup, and it turned into a disaster. The intention was pretty clear. We should increase sales so we can make more money, right? Unfortunately, this didn't drive my sales team forward. It wasn't that they didn't have motivation, it was that they didn't have *direction*.

Firstly, they didn't know what the target was that they needed to hit each month. One of my employees was happy to sign one client in the first month, but that wasn't exactly what we needed to drive our company forward. Moreover, the lack of progress from our sales team ended up leading to less revenue, and our administrative costs started to creep up on us.

I knew something was wrong, but it wasn't them. It came down to how I had set the standards for them. I basically gave them such a vague goal that they didn't know what standards were to be met, when they had to be met, or how they were going to be measured. Basically, everything deteriorated into confusion without concrete numbers and standards in place.

This is when I learned about another interesting approach to setting goals, and it is known as the SMART approach. The acronym stands for Specific, Measurable, Attainable, Relevant, and Time-Bound. This was another game-changing framework that transformed the dynamics of my business and helped us increase our revenue. Let's break down each one of the key aspects of SMART goals.

Be Specific

The first thing you need to keep in mind when you're setting goals is to be very specific. Make the goal as detailed as possible. This is where my "increase sales" shoutout came up short. An example of a specific goal would be: "Land client contracts worth over $5,000 in the first quarter" or "Increase sales from $500,000 in Year 1 to $1,000,000 in Year 2." Now that sounds more like it. With specific goals like these, you know what you are doing, and this provides your team with a direction and standards to aim for.

Make It Measurable

The next important goal-setting strategy is to ensure that they can be measured. Setting goals such as increasing sales from $500,000 to $1,000,000 in consecutive years won't mean anything if you don't know how to measure your progress. Hence, we need to break it down further into steps, such as know how many leads we need to generate per month and keep track of precise KPIs (Key Performance Indicators) to monitor the campaign's effectiveness. These things will help you measure your goals (more on measuring goals later in the chapter).

It Should Be Attainable

Another essential aspect of goal-setting is to aim for goals that can be achieved. In a nutshell, be realistic about your goals. Can you realistically achieve hitting sales numbers from $500,000 to $1,000,000 in a year? If so, then list out how it can be done and include things such as increasing lead funnels, re-aligning branding strategy, implementing more campaigns, etc.

It Must Be Relevant

Next up, your goals that you set should be relevant to your business. If your digital marketing goal consists of keeping track of the number of likes your social media posts get, then that's not really relevant. It's not relevant to how you can optimize your business growth and will simply lead you to waste time and resources in the wrong areas. Ensure your goals are relevant, such as finding ways to address the pain points of your customers, identifying areas where your service could deliver better satisfaction to clients, and other goals related to your digital marketing agency's success.

Make It Time-Bound

Every goal you set needs a deadline. Deadlines might not always be met, but having that guidepost will do a great deal to steer an individual forward to take action and complete tasks. When I pulled out that vague "increase sales" goal, there wasn't any deadline attached to it. Many were happy with signing one client per month, but they were unsure of whether this was what they needed to do to hit those sales goals. If you put a deadline on it, such as "Land client contracts worth over $5,000 in the first quarter," this urges employees to devise their individual strategies and use their skills and effort to achieve that target within the specified period.

Example

Let's put this into an example. Suppose you need to set goals not for your agency but for a digital marketing campaign for your client. This is where having this mindset can also help your clients and improve the reputation of your agency.

You are tasked with carrying out a social media marketing campaign, and the goal is specific. It's related to improving their Facebook page followers to promote their products and generate leads later on. Hence, you may set a goal this way:

"Ensure the Facebook page acquires over 20,000 followers by the end of the year and that the traffic to the client's company website increases by 25%."

Was it specific? It definitely was. I'm sure your marketing team knows what's expected of them, as this gives them clear direction.

Is it measurable? You can measure it, and this is where finding ways to measure the results of your social media marketing campaign comes into play, such as bringing in KPIs like clicks, engagement, hashtag performance, views, organic traffic, paid traffic, etc.

Is it attainable? In this market, and with the presence of advanced digital marketing tools, it sure is. This is where you can spark a good discussion with your team to identify the tools that will help you hit the target, such as bringing in AI tools for assistance or using better analytic dashboards for effective tracking of metrics.

Is it relevant? No doubt it will be when you break down your goals into small and manageable tasks that are relevant to your overall goals.

Is it time-bound? Absolutely. You need to achieve this by the end of the year, so your team has a target. Your client has also been given the expectation that they will see positive results by that time.

Planning Your Digital Marketing Budget

The next important thing I want to address is about your finances. A digital marketing agency needs to manage its finances wisely in order to see effective results and sustain profitable growth. This is where having a budget helps.

A digital marketing budget is essentially an overview of your income and expenditures. This is necessary to have for your business itself and also for managing your client's budget when you take on marketing campaigns.

Drafting an Effective Budget Plan

Creating a proper budget plan depends on your company goals and also the goals you set when you undertake client projects. Firstly, you will need to understand how much money you will be able to put aside and invest for a digital marketing project.

I make use of Microsoft Excel or Google Sheets to keep track of my budgeting plans in a spreadsheet (I use Google Sheets mostly now because it makes it easy to collaborate with my accountant).

For each project, create a budget for a specific period and make use of two columns: Budget and Actual. The Budget column lists the finances you have planned before the start of the project, and the Actual column is for the investments made throughout the project.

This will provide a real-time view for you to keep track of whether you are keeping up with your budget plan. This will also tell you when you need to reassess your strategy to ensure your finances aren't heading in the wrong direction.

Moreover, you have to make your budgeting plan as detailed as possible by listing the channels that you are using during the project. This will include things like social media platforms, emails, websites, the marketing tools/software you acquire or invest in, and also the manpower costs for the project, such as outsourcing services to freelancers, contractors, and so on.

During the initial years of my digital marketing agency, sticking to a budget plan helped me so much. There were times during certain projects where clients provided a limited budget, and we were able to identify through the budgeting plan that investing in advanced marketing tools was not going to help us fulfill the client's goals within their budget.

Hence, this encouraged us to employ other strategies, such as focusing less on marketing and leveraging one or two other channels to get the client the best conversion rates. In addition, doing more organic-style marketing, such as blogging on the client's website (as we have some exceptional writers on our team), helped us present SEO-rich content.

As a result, a couple of these strategies helped to improve organic traffic without the need to invest in paid ads, since that costs more.

Tips for Making Better Budget Plans

Here are a few more tips that can help you make better budgeting plans internally and also when working on marketing projects for clients:

- Use the 70-20-10 rule, where 70% of your budget is spent on strategies that you have used frequently and that work well, 20% goes to strategies that are new but still effective, and 10% goes to experimental strategies that you can explore.
- Keep track of your costs on a regular basis, including employee salaries, digital marketing campaign costs, and other miscellaneous costs, to optimize your budget plan.
- Make sure your budget plan aligns with your marketing goals and doesn't affect the business's growth plans.
- Monitor your business's sales cycle and revenue regularly to identify whether you can afford to allocate larger portions of the budget.
- Go through your past strategies to see what worked and didn't work, and then utilize the processes that made your campaigns run smoothly.
- Consider contingency plans and external factors that could possibly alter your budget plan, including holidays, special events, economic crises, and even

the weather if this could impact your daily operations.

Measuring Your Digital Marketing Goals

Identifying and setting goals along with planning an effective budget is all well and good, but without monitoring and measuring your progress, you may soon experience problems. Measuring goals helps you know where you stand—whether you are moving closer to achieving your goal or moving further away from it. In digital marketing, the performance of your marketing campaigns determines your success in achieving your goals, either for your clients or internally.

Know Your KPIs

One fine way that digital marketing teams measure progress is utilizing KPIs. A KPI is a Key Performance Indicator and is a numerical metric that helps to measure the progress of a marketing campaign, channel, or defined goal.

Here are a few important KPIs you need to know about and incorporate when you measure goals:

- **MQL to SQL Conversion Rate**: Marketing Qualified Leads (MQL) is a digital marketing metric for measuring generated lead volume by marketing initiatives. Sales Qualified Leads are qualified prospects defined by the sales team. Hence, MQL to SQL conversion rates are utilized to measure the number of MQLs that convert to SQLs.
- **Customer Acquisition Cost (CAC)**: This is a metric used by both sales and marketing teams to measure the costs incurred when acquiring a new client. This

provides good insight as far as the cost of acquiring a specific customer to leverage certain profitable customer segments.

- **Customer Lifetime Value (CLV)**: As this was discussed in-depth in the previous chapter, you probably don't need another introduction to its importance. This is also used as an insightful metric to measure marketing and sales goals.
- **Return on Ad Spend (ROAS)**: This indicates the revenue generated for each dollar invested in advertising campaigns. It helps you to identify the advertising campaigns that are contributing to profits and those that are incurring losses.
- **Impressions**: This is a metric that measures the number of times a webpage, social media post, ad campaign, etc., is viewed. It helps you measure your campaign's visibility factor and ascertain whether it is reaching the right target audience.
- **Goal Completions**: The goal completion metric provides you with insight on the number of customers converting to accomplish specific goals. For instance, it might measure the number of visitors to your landing page that convert to paying customers. It helps you understand a marketing strategy's effectiveness.
- **Click-Through Rate (CTR)**: You've probably heard of this already, as it is a commonly valued metric in digital marketing. It measures how often visitors are prompted to click on your site when it is displayed on SERPs (Search Engine Result Pages) and navigate to it. This metric can be used in digital marketing campaigns—from email marketing to social media content. The higher the CTR, the better

the indication that you're reaching your target audience.

- **Traffic by Channels**: This is an insightful metric used to identify marketing channels from which you are getting the most traffic to your website, landing page, etc. Hence, this will tell you if you are getting traffic from channels such as emails, social media platforms, organic visitors, direct visitors, paid visitors, referrals, etc.

- **Website Visits**: As the name suggests, this metric measures the total number of people who visit your website/webpage during a specific period and helps you understand where they are coming from.

- **Interactions per Visit**: This analyzes visitors' interactions with the visual content and other components of your web page. This helps you understand your audience's user experience and preferences.

- **Average Time on a Page**: This metric analyzes the average amount of time a visitor spends on your webpage. You can see this when you use Google Analytics, and it helps you learn whether your visitors are spending time reading your content.

- **Bounce Rate**: This refers to the number of visitors who visit your website and immediately leave without interacting at all with your page. When you see a high bounce rate, this indicates that you are reaching the wrong audience, your content is not exactly meeting their needs, or you are failing to address their pain points.

- **Exit Rate**: This measures the number of visitors who leave the website from a specific page. It can be an important metric to understand where your site's flaws are and how they are keeping visitors from converting into paying customers.

- **Content Engagement**: This is an essential metric that helps you track and measure user engagement with your content. For instance, for a social media post, it helps to measure the likes, comments, clicks, and shares to help you determine how engaging your content is.

- **Inbound Links**: As part of the link-building strategy, this metric measures the number of inbound links to your website. This is an important part that utilizes Google's algorithm to promote your website to higher placements in SERPs.

- **Cost per Visitor (CPV)**: This measures the total investment made from any marketing effort that acquired a single visitor.

- **Revenue per Visitor (RPV)**: This measures the revenue earned per visitor. Your RPV, measured with your CPV, helps you understand your marketing initiatives' effectiveness. For instance, if your RPV is higher than your CPV, then it's a profitable sign. If the reverse is the case, it indicates you need to reassess your marketing efforts.

- **Net Promoter Score (NPS)**: This is a useful metric utilized to measure your customers' loyalty by asking them how likely they would be to recommend your company to another person. Out of a rating scale of 0–10 (10 being the highest), true promoters —those who are primed to spread the word about your company—often lie between 9 and 10. Passive promoters, usually a mixed type of promoter (sometimes they will promote, sometimes they won't), lie between 7 and 8. Finally, those who rate below 7 are seen as detractors, or those who are unlikely to spread the word about your company.

Knowing these KPIs is crucial when you run a digital marketing agency. They help you to measure your goals properly and ensure you have the best chance of meeting them.

For instance, if your goal is to increase organic traffic to your company website (or your client's) by 25% within 2–3 months, then you know you have to analyze metrics such as Traffic by Channel, Website Visits, Interactions per Visit, Impressions, CTR, etc., to know whether you are effectively reaching your target audience.

When it comes to your content strategy for your website, you can analyze the Content Engagement score, Average Time on a Page, Bounce Rate, Exit Rate, Inbound links, etc., to know how well you're hooking visitors to stay on your site.

Moreover, when it comes to your budgeting needs, you can analyze the CPV, RPV, ROAS, and CAC to understand how effective these marketing campaigns are working to meet your budget and meet your goals.

Key Takeaways From This Chapter

- Making goals and measuring them helps your digital marketing business to scale and grow to another level.
- Identify your digital marketing goals by making use of the five Ss—Sell, Speak, Serve, Save, and Sizzle.
- Set effective digital marketing goals by utilizing the SMART approach—make it Specific, Measurable, Attainable, Relevant, and Time-bound.

- A digital marketing budget plan helps you manage your finances properly, both internally and during client projects. It provides an overview of your income and expenditures and provides a real-time view to track and monitor actual spending versus budgeted spending.
- To make an effective budgeting plan, one strategy you can utilize is the 70-20-10 rule: 70% of the budget goes toward strategies that you have used frequently and that work well, 20% toward strategies that are new but still effective, and 10% goes to experimental strategies.
- You can measure digital marketing goals by making use of KPIs. It is essential to know the different metrics involved to help you measure specific digital marketing goals and manage campaigns successfully.

Chapter 3

Client Acquisition – Targeting the Right Clients for Your Business

Get closer than ever to your customers. So close, in fact, that you tell them what they need well before they realize it themselves.

— Steve Jobs

L et's move on and focus on acquiring your ideal clients for your agency in order to make a profit and meet your business's goals. I've seen many entrepreneurs make one common mistake, and that is going out there without a plan, acting desperate, and trying to please everyone.

This not only wins you fewer customers, it also makes it challenging to work with them in the long run. That's why this chapter will help you determine who your ideal client should be when you are offering your services, as well as how you can land clients who will depend on your agency.

Eventually, this will help you build a stream of qualified leads coming through your marketing funnel. You will end up working with clients who are the right fit for you and them. After all, that's what a healthy business relationship is all about. It's about chemistry and ensuring both parties can collaborate with each other successfully.

Determining Your Target Client

The first step in our client acquisition process is to determine who your ideal client is. This is an essential step in your process of finding quality clients. Keep in mind how I mentioned a while ago that many entrepreneurs make the common mistake of overlooking this aspect. For instance, I committed the same mistake when I started my agency.

I was desperate to find *anyone* and wanted to get my business off the ground quickly—mainly because I wanted to recoup my investment costs as soon as possible. I'm sure any entrepreneur, and even yourself, could end up in this situation, where your emotions dominate your decision-making.

It happened to me, and we spent our time, money, and resources trying to please anyone we found and ended up only signing two clients that we couldn't even work with. One reason for this was that they only agreed to a very low rate for the projects, since they were startups themselves, and second, they weren't transparent enough with us, as they were less committed to our working relationship and kept delaying our project for weeks for no good reason.

Eventually, this took a toll on our revenue, and we ended up taking a loss for a couple of months for all that hard work of going out in the market and trying to please everyone. This is when we decided to be strategic in our client acquisition approach and to target clients who were suited to our business. First, we needed to ask ourselves who we were looking for to meet our specific goals.

Developing a Customer Avatar

Defining our potential and ideal client was the first step to solving our problems. This was made possible by creating our unique customer avatar. A customer avatar is basically a representation of your ideal client that describes their characteristics as if they are a fictional character. Hence, me and my team sat down one day and discussed our ideal client by using a whiteboard and a marker.

We took turns going up to the whiteboard and writing down characteristics of our ideal client who we would love to work with; someone who would meet our financial goals. We gave them a simple name, such as John/Jane, and started thinking of three or four characteristics that met our business goals and the services we provided.

Just to share an example, we determined our customer avatar or target client to be the following:

Name: John/Jane Doe

Age: Late 30s

Occupation: Marketing manager

Company size: Medium-sized businesses (at least 50 employees)

Their boss: CEO, VP of Marketing

Industry: B2B (Business-to-Business), SaaS (Software-as-a-Service)

Location: U.S. and Canada

Interests: Want to elevate the business's marketing strategy, establish online presence, develop frequent content.

Pain points: Lack of time and in-house team to run digital marketing campaigns, busy with running offline promotions and events, etc.

As you can see from this example, this gave us a direction for finding clients who matched the profile, or were similar. This helped us to focus our marketing efforts on finding these types of clients and getting quality leads who would be interested in our services and also agree to a rate that met our financial goals.

You can use this for inspiration, but remember, you don't need to follow the same client profile when focusing on your own digital marketing agency. For instance, you may be based somewhere else, for starters, or you might be offering different services with different market conditions.

Moreover, at each stage of your digital marketing agency, your goals may fluctuate. An agency that has zero clients cannot land corporations with over a hundred employees easily when competing with established agencies that have a wider customer base. Hence, you should learn what your agency needs and determine to whom you can successfully deliver your services to make better profits.

Narrowing Down a Market Through Segmentation

The above example is a great exercise to use if you are just starting out and don't have a single client yet. If you are a bit more established or have a decent customer base, you can implement criteria that will help you to narrow down your preferred target clients through segmentation; that is, splitting your customer base into smaller segments.

For example, your criteria could depend on the following:

- business type
- size of the company
- products/services
- geographical location
- pain points

This is a good start, especially since you are running a B2B company. We applied the same segmentation criteria six months into our startup journey to narrow down the clients we would most likely bring in more revenue from.

We found out that the majority of clients fit the following description:

Business type: SaaS businesses

Size of the company: Corporations that have between 30 and 100 employees (You can acquire this information by telling them to fill out a KYC form or looking up the company online)

Products/Services: Work-related/office-based productivity online tools

Geographical location: Mostly from western parts of the U.S.

Pain points: Trying to launch new products/features in a competitive marketplace, no in-house digital marketing team to run and manage campaigns.

The positive of this study was that it helped us to focus our marketing and keep targeting these specific sets of customers so that we could have a steady funnel of quality leads coming through.

Moreover, it was easy for us to build that momentum and sign these clients because we already had a portfolio and testimonials from clients who matched the profile, and this convinced them that we were reliable enough to deliver results for them.

Building a Lead Generating Machine: Marketing Funnel

As a digital marketing agency, your job is to deliver marketing results for your clients. Likewise, you have to apply the same process in your own marketing efforts to land clients in the first place. To ensure a consistent stream of revenue, you will require a continuous stream of leads coming through.

Let's be honest; you could be generating 500+ leads in a specific period, but only 50 may get through as qualified leads, 10 get through to engage in several meetings with you, and only 1 or 2 end up signing with you. As you can now see, that's the reality, and this means you need a lot of leads flowing through your business consistently to land more paying clients. This is the reality of business, but if you have a process and workflow that is ready to generate many leads, then you shouldn't have to worry too much.

Establishing Your Customer Journey

A customer journey refers to your prospect's first-ever interaction with your business, and this follows all the way to when they either purchase your services and work with you or disengage from your business.

In theory, a marketing funnel helps to identify five major components that can help you strategically tailor your marketing messages to your prospects at different significant stages. You need to fill the funnel by generating qualified leads so that you can keep trying to convert them into customers.

Here is a breakdown of the five components of a marketing funnel:

1. Awareness

The first stage is the awareness stage, and this is where your prospect or potential customer becomes aware of your company or brand through your marketing efforts. For example, my agency used paid ads on Facebook and LinkedIn to display ads that targeted our best prospects.

The more and more they saw the ad on their feed, the more they became aware of what we do. Other examples may include producing content such as blog posts, infographics, videos, podcasts, etc., so that people become aware of your brand and you are no longer a stranger.

2. Consideration

This stage focuses on when you start engaging with the prospect and then offer your services. This includes your typical sales process (will be covered later in this chapter) and understanding the prospect's requirements and pain points. You then give them the option to consider buying your service.

For example, my agency used emails to first engage with prospects for a discovery call. Then we were able to land meetings over the phone, in person, and through video conferences. We crafted our messages so that they were tailored for this stage and got prospects into a position to sign with us.

3. Purchase

This is the conversion stage. If your prospect has reached this stage, then you were successful in getting them to sign with you. (Your marketing messages will differ here, as will your operations.)

For example, when a client signs with my agency, we send a welcome email immediately listing what's expected in our business relationship and how we will be working on the first project, including details about the deliverables. Then we follow up by scheduling several meetings to confirm project details, report on our progress, and conduct on-premises visits if needed.

4. Retention

This stage focuses on establishing customer loyalty. Hence, you should be crafting messages and campaigns that encourage your customers to build trust and loyalty with you.

Due to intense competition, it is easy for a customer to switch to another agency even if they have a long-term contract they have signed with you. It's the harsh truth of business, and it is up to you to deliver using strategies that will keep your current customers close.

For example, my agency focuses on optimizing our service model so that we keep providing the best experience to our clients. We also provide in-depth reports and analyses that keep clients happy with their marketing campaign's progress. Moreover, we follow up with them personally after each project and ask about their business growth before introducing new services that are tailor-made for the market and their requirements.

5. Advocacy

This last stage focuses on your customer's willingness to spread the word about your brand or agency. It can be positive or negative, but this indicates how well you are establishing a brand name and also determines the number of clients that you can potentially sign in the long run.

You should focus on driving your customers toward spreading positive feedback and reviews about your business. For example, my agency checks in with our customers occasionally to ask them for referrals. We also use our company social media accounts to promote content and urge our audience to share posts and refer our services to their friends who may have need for us with their business.

Following this model will help you to strategize your marketing messages according to each stage, but it will also help fill in qualified leads to fuel your business's growth and long-term income potential.

Finding Clients: Know Your Sources

So far, you have learned how to create a specific customer profile so that you can target the right clients for your agency. In addition, the marketing funnel framework can help you strategize your marketing messages accordingly. Next up, you may be wondering, "Where can I find these clients?"

Here are a few reliable sources that helped me. They may also help you find many leads and potential customers that fit your profile:

- Online directories

The first source is pretty old-fashioned but still effective. It is using directories. Nowadays, you can utilize online directories to find small-to-medium-sized businesses that you are targeting. Most online directories will provide you with ample information, such as the contact numbers of these businesses and sometimes their email addresses. I mainly use YellowPages. I simply type the keyword, such as its niche, and also the location where I want it based. You can also make use of other online directories like WhitePages, Manta, and Yelp.

- Website scraping

The next source involves two steps. First, search on Google for companies by entering keywords and the location. For example, "candy shops in Los Angeles, CA" or "Software companies in Austin, TX." You can find the websites of these companies this way. The next step is to install website extraction or scraping tools that allow you to add them as an extension to your browser. This helps you to extract the email addresses of the people working for that company. For instance, if you visit a company website, you will find an option on your browser to use your website scraping tool, and it will display several email addresses of people to build your email list and contact them. I make use of Getemail.io and Snov.io extensions to extract information from company websites.

- Google

Google is a great source for finding clients when you first start out. You can use the last step and search keywords to get access to different company names. From there, you can collect each company's name and contact details and store this on your prospecting list. In addition, you can use Google's search algorithm to get your website ranked higher in the SERPs (Search Engine Result Pages) and help clients find you. This is done by optimizing your website for SEO purposes through incorporating important keywords in your website content that clients search for frequently, including internal and external links, and making your website well-curated for reading. However, this route can take time, and especially for a startup, you need quicker results. Hence, you can utilize Google Ads (formerly known as Google Adwords) and have your company website displayed when potential clients search for your services on Google. Google Ads can make your company stand out more, for a fee, as it will put your site in front of other people looking to optimize their website's search visibility organically.

- LinkedIn

Indeed, social media is a great source to find leads, but nothing is as good as LinkedIn. I've leveraged this platform for our agency's marketing strategy, and it has paid off well. You can utilize LinkedIn by directly reaching out to potential clients by searching keywords using LinkedIn's search—which I find to be on the same level as Google for its search efficiency. You can join groups, publish articles, and build an audience of prospects who will reach out to you in due time. In addition, you can buy a Premium membership and unlock features for reaching out to clients, such as more private messaging options, running paid ads that can reach your prospects' LinkedIn feeds, and also access to the LinkedIn Sales Navigator—a LinkedIn sales-oriented tool that helps you find prospects that match your customer avatar and generate tons of leads.

- Facebook

The next important social media platform that can still be used to bring you good leads is Facebook. Facebook is not only a place to casually connect with friends, it is also a place to do business. As the largest social media platform in the world, Facebook provides the opportunity to target plenty of prospects by joining groups, reaching out to them privately, and running Facebook Ads that will reach your prospects' feeds. When compared to LinkedIn, Facebook's marketing tools are cheaper in cost when it comes to its cost-per-click, so this is a good tool if you have a limited budget when starting out.

- YouTube

YouTube is probably the second-best search engine platform after Google. Our agency leveraged this platform. We have creative people on our team who are passionate about making videos and have a bunch of great ideas. Each week, we published two videos that provided educational content, such as why companies need a digital marketing agency and the different types of digital marketing campaigns a company needs. This helped us to rank our content thanks to YouTube's search algorithm. People watched our videos and then reached out to us. The best part of YouTube is that your video will be on the platform for years getting more and more views. So, a video you published in 2023 could still be getting views in 2027, and those people will still reach out to you if they are interested. Moreover, you can also run YouTube ads to target specific prospects that fit your digital marketing customer profile.

- Guest Blogging

Guest blogging is the act of posting on someone else's website. This helps you gain exposure and visibility for your company, as well as establish an online presence and credibility for the expertise you offer. For instance, you can write guest blogs on digital marketing-related websites to provide educational content and also increase your brand awareness. Potential clients will find you by either visiting the website and finding your guest blog or searching on Google and seeing relevant content that connects to your guest post.

- Quora

Similar to guest blogging, Quora is another platform where you can find prospects looking for answers to their questions. Most of these are pain points, and oftentimes they are looking for a digital marketing-related solution. Hence, if you sign up on Quora as your company account and start answering questions, you can gain exposure and visibility on Quora. Google will also promote these types of entities on the search engine when potential clients search relevant keywords online.

- Networking Conferences and Events

This source can be utilized either online or through offline means. Attending workshops, events, trade shows, conferences, etc., can help you gain exposure for your brand and let everyone know that you have arrived in the market. You can register for online workshops, meet other digital marketers, and connect with them or potential prospects in the industry. You can also go offline and attend networking events. Simply search on Google or ask your contacts and you will soon find some near you that you can attend. Moreover, you can participate in these events by working on your public speaking and talking about your expertise in your field. This will help you build rapport, and people will come to you asking for your number and may potentially buy your agency's services.

- Access to Databases

Getting access to databases of digital marketing prospects is an effective way to build your email list and reach out to potential customers. This is another old-fashioned method similar to using online directories, and it involves buying access to these databases. Hence, it can be an expensive route compared to the other sources discussed above. So, if you have a limited budget as you start out, I wouldn't prioritize investing in this source alone. Many of the sources above are much more cost-effective.

Making Clients Come to You

The previous section provided you with sources where you can reach out to clients to start understanding their pain points and pitch your services. Even though this can be an effective strategy, cold outreach can be time-consuming, too, and challenging to your team's temperament. Hence, you will also need to master the skill of attracting clients to you by collecting inbound leads.

Inbound marketing includes strategies to make clients come to you instead of the other way around. This is made possible by increasing your brand awareness and online presence. Moreover, assessing your current marketing strategies and looking from a potential client's perspective can help you identify where you may have room for improvement.

There is a good practice that we implemented for our marketing team, and that is to see ourselves as a client and conduct marketing activities to convince ourselves. Yes, you read that right! It might sound peculiar when you read it again, but I assure you, this works. If you can spot where you have compromised on quality and pitched unconvincing marketing messages to yourself, then you have a clear picture of what you need to work on. If you can't impress yourself, then your potential clients won't be impressed at all.

Because, let's be real; if you can't do the marketing right for your business's benefit, how can you expect clients to trust that you will do a good job marketing their business? It all starts with you.

Here are other effective tips you can use to build credibility for your agency and attract more clients over the long term:

Optimize the Company's Portfolio

As you know, the competition is intense, and so are your potential clients' inboxes. They receive the same messages from thousands of providers like you saying how great they are in digital marketing and how they can solve any problem. But what makes you stand out from others is showing them your work and the actual proof that you can solve their problems.

This is where having an updated online portfolio helps to display your firm's credentials, certificates, clients you have worked with, testimonials, and proof of work delivered through case studies. A case study basically consists of information regarding the client you worked with, the problem they had, the solution you provided (your specific digital marketing service), and the results they achieved (usually a positive one that transformed their business).

Online portfolios are also a great way to tailor your presentation to specific target clients. For instance, over time, if you want to attract more clients in a specific niche, like the woodworking industry, you can update your online portfolio to show off past woodworking clients for whom you delivered great results. This provides them with enough information to be impressed by your expertise, and it is also relevant to them and their industry. This will make it more likely that they will reach out to you to start discussing business.

Leverage the Power of Content

Providing content through various channels is another effective way to attract clients by showing that you are an expert in what you do and providing educational content to increase your brand awareness. You can distribute content in a few different ways.

The most common and cost-effective method is blogging. You can use your company website to maintain a blog where you frequently publish articles related to solving your prospects' particular pain points. Your potential prospects find your articles by searching keywords on Google and checking the results pages. If you optimize your website to make it SEO-efficient, then you will increase your chances of being found through Google by these prospects.

Another way to distribute content is through social channels. Make accounts on LinkedIn, Facebook, Instagram, etc., or social platforms where you will find your target prospects online, and distribute content there. It can be articles, short posts providing educational content, infographics, or video content.

Videos are probably the most effective form of content besides blogs, and if you have an expert video editor on your team, like my team does, you can easily leverage video marketing to increase your brand awareness. You can also make use of YouTube to leverage its algorithm and make your videos visible to potential clients.

Engage and Educate Clients to Establish Authority

To make yourself stand out as the ultimate option, you must be good at engaging your potential prospects and educating them. A combination of these two actions helps to build authority, and this alone can attract many clients to your agency in the long run.

When brands master the social aspect of things, they find they are more successful with getting more clients compared to those who overlook the importance of engaging with their audience. I know it can be time-consuming to constantly check your social media accounts and react to each comment and query, but in our agency, we were pretty organized with this.

Firstly, we had a couple of members who were in charge of handling all the interactions on social media and other platforms. Secondly, there was a scheduled time to do it. We had a routine; for instance, every other day, we would engage with our audience on Facebook and Instagram and respond to their queries. Additionally, when it came to responding to emails from our newsletter subscribers, we batched them to only respond after 4 p.m. every day. We didn't check on Sundays. This is, of course, separate from the emails our sales team got, which they would respond to immediately when a client reached out.

The real power of engaging with your audience on social media on a regular basis manifests later on when you are ready to approach them. After you've built rapport on social media, it won't feel like cold outreach. In fact, the potential prospect will be aware of you and will know your brand well from the constant engagement, so it will feel more like a warm approach.

Since we had creative writers with a strong work ethic, we also engaged followers by sending them weekly email newsletters. We provided newsletters for free to subscribers for at least three months and sent brief digital marketing-related content that could help their business. It was an encouraging thing to do for us because we actually received positive responses from it. After three months, we would then ask them to pay a small fee to keep receiving exclusive email newsletter content. In the long run, we were able to get a few paying clients who were subscribers. This is an underrated method to get clients because most businesses just don't have the patience to send newsletters to their followers—especially for free or at minimum charge.

All these methods above help you to not only engage with your potential clients but also educate them. To dive further into the educating game, offering webinars to a group of people is also a good way to establish some authority and build rapport. People look up to experts who can provide them with valuable knowledge that transforms their lives. If you can educate your audience and provide value, you will be sure to build trust with them and also win a few clients from the crowd.

If you have a content team that can manage creating digital marketing courses, then you can sell these on sites like Udemy to get potential clients or referrals that way. Because education is powerful and people like to spread the word to others when they find valuable content, your course could go viral and win you more clients. Suddenly you and your agency will be industry experts, your sales meetings will go smoother because they are aware of what you can bring to the table, and the pressure of closing a deal will be eased.

Organizing Your Resources to Be Seen as the Expert

All the avenues I have mentioned so far come from our experiences of being able to establish authority in our niche market and shift from a sales-resisting, cold outreach to a warm, inbound marketing machine. If you can get your agency to automatically run in inbound marketing mode after a year or two, then you are going to enjoy this business more and have more free time (in addition to the obvious perk of earning more revenue).

For that, you need to organize a few key resources that should be part of your inbound marketing strategy, and these resources will help you to expose yourself as the expert in your niche and encourage people to come to you based on what you provide or how you inspire them. In this way, you will find your sales conversion rate is higher compared to when you do cold outreach every time.

Here are a few digital resources that can help you communicate your expertise:

- **Ebooks**: This is a great way to exhibit your knowledge and your expertise on a topic. Focus on writing and marketing short- or long-form ebooks regarding digital marketing-related topics in your niche that help solve some common pain points in your market. This way, when prospects like your ebook, you will find them coming to you and mentioning straight off the bat that they read your ebook and liked your advice.
- **Podcasts**: If you are a great speaker, or have a team of great speakers, then you might enjoy doing podcast episodes. It is easy to air your podcast on platforms such as Spotify and BuzzSprout. Be articulate and deliver tons of episodes providing advice and expertise in your niche; people will come to you when they see you as the expert.
- **Case Studies**: I mentioned the importance of case studies earlier in this chapter and demonstrated how to structure them. Displaying them on your website helps illustrate to clients the complex projects you have worked on. In addition, written and video testimonials can help to boost that credibility as well.
- **Guides**: A guide is another useful way to establish some expertise in your niche. Create guides that educate your audience, and be sure it isn't just basic content. For example, provide guides for your

audience to teach them step-by-step how to properly run Google Ads campaigns, or teach them about various software tools that they can use to automate their digital marketing workflow. These are the kinds of guides you should aim for rather than writing on general topics.

- **Webinars**: Hosting people through webinars and teaching them about various things in your niche using video-conferencing tools can help you to engage with prospects and display your expertise.
- **Public Speaking**: You have probably seen people coming on TEDx and giving inspiring speeches on their expertise. This is another influential way to communicate your expertise to your audience. I'm not saying you need to get yourself up on TEDx and give a speech (though you can always try; you never know!), but you could search for venues or online platforms where you can provide speeches and present your authority to an audience.

Converting Prospects to Clients

We will end the chapter by going through briefly the sales process that you must incorporate with your sales team. This should be a robust process, and your team should have the mindset of tenacity to overcome hurdles and stay hungry to close more deals.

Here are the steps involved in a typical sales process, and following this can help you strategically organize your messages and actions in order to get prospects down the sales funnel and eventually convert them into your clients.

1. Prospecting

The earlier sections covered the prospecting step and how you can find and attract potential clients for your lead list. Your marketing efforts can help make things easier for your sales team when you implement the marketing strategies outlined in this chapter and add them to your arsenal. In summary, prospecting is the act of qualifying potential clients and evaluating whether they require your services or not.

2. Initial Contact

Your first contact can come in different ways, but the end goal of this step is only one thing—book a meeting with the prospect. You might reach out to them by sending cold emails asking them to book a discovery call with you. You might directly call these companies, or even visit them. I wouldn't recommend the latter too frequently, especially when you visit big corporations, as they will likely be annoyed by this. But if your target clients are small-business owners, shops, etc., then an unannounced visit might bring you unexpected and positive results.

3. Pre-Meeting Rituals

After you have successfully booked a first meeting with them, you or your sales team will spend some time doing further research and learning more about your potential client. Draft some questions that you would like to ask them that are tailored to their business and will encourage them to open up to you regarding their pain points. Plan your routes efficiently if your prospect is based far away from your location so you can reach the meeting on time, or else ensure your video-conferencing tools are in good condition if it is an online meeting.

4. The Meeting

The meeting is all about conversing with your prospects and understanding more about their business and pain points. Once you have the information, you can start your presentation and demonstrate how your digital-marketing services will help them solve their problems. Even though this can be done by one person, it is always good to have your sales team attend meetings in pairs so they can support each other and ensure the presentation goes well.

5. Addressing Objections

The next phase can happen either during the first meeting or after a series of meetings, because most of the time, you cannot close a deal on your first attempt like you see in the movies. It doesn't work that way. Your clients will have a series of objections, and you should be prepared to handle and address them efficiently. The more you know about your services and have faith in them, the more likely you will be to handle these objections well. Of course, price negotiation is a different kettle of fish, but if you can convince them and make them *want* your service, then price isn't going to be much of an objection from their side.

6. Closing

The closing stage involves your potential client's decision to go forward in the process. It can be either positive or negative. They could say no and the deal is closed there, or they could say yes, and you have a new client. Your closing process should involve negotiating how payment terms will be applied (for instance, is it full payment up front, or 50% pre-service and 50% after the project is completed?), any offers or benefits they can avail from working with you, and planning the long-term business relationship with your agency by signing a contract.

7. Follow Up

After you have signed your client, continue communicating regularly with them. Ensure that their needs are being met, and then you can request feedback regarding how you're conducting business for them. You may also ask them for referrals when it's appropriate. Simply calling and checking up on them helps you to build a strong bond, and this helps you to retain your customers long-term. A common mistake business owners make is that they think once they sign the client, it's in the bag, but at any moment, your competitors can easily take them away from you. Therefore, you must always have that in mind and keep your current customers close.

Key Takeaways From This Chapter

- Determine the right client to target by developing a customer avatar that shows exactly the characteristics and profile of the client that fits your business.
- Establish a marketing funnel that helps you to tailor your marketing messages during each stage. The five

components are awareness, consideration, purchase, retention, and advocacy.

- You can find digital marketing clients from many sources, such as online directories, Google, website scraping, social media platforms, YouTube, Quora, networking events, and buying access to databases.
- You can build authority and attract more clients by optimizing your company's portfolio for credibility, producing content regularly, engaging with your audience, and educating them.
- A few digital resources that help you to communicate your expertise are ebooks, podcasts, case studies, testimonials, guides, webinars, and public speaking events.
- Your typical sales process to convert prospects to clients includes prospecting, initial contact, pre-meeting rituals, meeting/presentation, addressing objections, closing, and follow-up.

Chapter 4

The Irrefusable Offer — What Do I Sell?

Don't pay attention to those who offer too much.

— Dejan Stojanovic

The previous chapter taught you ways to search for potential clients and land them for your digital marketing agency.

In this chapter, you will learn more by understanding what you can sell and how to deliver results to your clients. We'll go over a few concepts for how you can optimize your business for growth.

Additionally, you will learn the important digital marketing services you can provide to your client, the benefits of focusing on a specific niche, and how to productize your digital marketing services to scale your business and generate more revenue while enhancing your brand image.

Digital Marketing Services You Can Offer

First and foremost, let us go through a list of digital marketing services that your agency can offer to your customers. As a startup, it can be overwhelming to do everything and please everyone, so in the next section, you will learn the importance of niching down. However, it is best to be aware of the different services your agency can offer in this field.

You might have heard of many of these already if you did your research before reading this book, but you will find some services that are not so common and may play an integral part in your future clients' demands. Let's go through each:

Search Engine Optimization

Search Engine Optimization, or SEO, is the process of boosting your traffic to your website organically, or without paid ads. The goal of SEO is to increase the visibility of your website or page in the search engine so that potential clients can find you. You can offer this service to your clients as well so that they can attract potential clients to their businesses. Fortunately, most common website builders like Squarespace, Wix, and WordPress have built-in SEO tools for you to leverage, but it is essential to know how you can organically increase traffic.

There are on-page SEO services, such as improving the website's content by publishing blog posts with relevant keywords, landing pages, and so on. Then, you have off-page SEO services, such as optimizing the website externally by utilizing link-building strategies, or more simply put, including internal and external links. Internal links are links that take you from one web page to another on the same website. Whereas external links are links that take you from one website to another website with high credibility. Lastly, technical SEO are more complex services, such as optimizing the website's servers, allowing bots to crawl, and indexing the site.

Paid Advertising

Paid advertising involves—no surprise—paying to run ads online. The most common is Search Engine Marketing, or SEM, which is the process of buying ad space on the search engine results pages. It's basically the opposite of SEO as explained earlier. You are boosting traffic to your or your client's websites by paying money this way.

A popular payment method of paid ads is pay-per-click, or in short, PPC. You are required to pay a small fee each time an ad gets clicked. This can be an effective strategy if you are selling high-end services. If your package is priced between $500 and $1,000, then there is no harm in paying one or two dollars for a click that may result in a big sale like that. Definitely worth the investment.

Your ads can come in different forms, such as having sponsored ads (basically paid ads) on top of Google search engine results pages when potential clients enter relevant keywords, images, or even videos. The most common examples of ads you see online include online shopping carousel ads displayed on ecommerce sites or marketplaces, image or video display ads, and ads on social media feeds.

Content Marketing

As you are now familiar from the previous chapter, content is powerful, and we love to consume content on a daily basis.

Your and your client's websites are not complete without content. Hence, content marketing is the process of distributing content online.

This can include distributing content by publishing articles, blog posts, infographics, case studies, press releases, white papers, ebooks, videos, etc. Even the content you put out in your sales emails and newsletters falls under this category.

Your social media posts also serve as tools to deliver a powerful message to communicate your brand or share content from your landing page when looking to convert visitors to paying customers.

Additionally, hosting webinars and producing podcast episodes are modern-day content marketing techniques that can help you increase brand awareness and deliver results for your client to attract their own target clients. The most common channels to distribute content, both organic and paid, are through blogging, social media (or social media ads), and Google Ads.

Email Marketing

Emails are still powerful when used properly. Just about everyone has an email address where they can be reached. And emails provide you with ample time to devise a strategy that can convince your prospect. Email marketing is the process of promoting a business through email by getting recipients on board as subscribers.

You start off by publishing a lead magnet on social media or on any platform. A lead magnet's goal is to acquire essential information from a potential client; in this case, their email address. A lead magnet can be any content you provide for free, such as ebooks, case studies, whitepapers, and so on.

Once you get them to opt in, you have an email list of subscribers. You can schedule email regularly and provide your subscribers with news regarding your business, such as new products/services, important news, more valuable content, webinars, courses, special offers, and much more. As a result, this builds rapport with your audience, and some percentage of them will likely convert to paying customers.

Video Marketing

In the past, many businesses thought that having videos was an add-on or a luxury. But that's not the case anymore. Videos have become an integral part of a business's online marketing strategy, and video marketing requires the attention it deserves. Video creation involves powerful storytelling capacity, and this can be mastered by practicing scriptwriting, producing video content that is relevant, organizing clips, and editing the footage to make a good story.

For marketing purposes, creating short- and long-form videos that provide educational content, promotional content, and new product releases can help to boost a business's chance of getting and retaining clients.

Aside from marketing purposes, your clients could ask for video expertise from your agency for aspects of their own businesses, such as creating videos for onboarding, training tutorials, tutorials for using a specific tool or software, or webinar content.

Social Media Marketing

Social Media Marketing, or SMM, is the process of marketing through social media channels to promote a brand or business. As we know, social media is one of the most effective ways to reach clients and build a large audience.

Social media marketing will help you boost brand awareness on social media channels, establish a brand voice and presence online, utilize organic and paid techniques to promote your brand, engage with potential clients and audiences, and much more.

It is simply much easier to distribute content and marketing materials through social media platforms when compared to offline methods like billboards, magazines, etc. Moreover, one can leverage social media by researching more on the target audience and competitors and getting insight into market trends. Moreover, it can take a lot of eyes and hands to manage social media accounts consistently across many platforms. Hence, digital marketing clients tend to demand a lot of this particular service from agencies.

Public Relations Marketing

Public Relations, or PR Marketing in short, is essential for companies that are looking to establish an image and communicate their organizational values to the public. That's where a good PR team comes to the rescue, and your agency can provide this service as well.

Your agency can carry out initiatives online to promote your client's upcoming event or strategize their brand image online by incorporating innovative brand-building ad campaigns, webinars, workshops, public interviews, and much more.

Performance Marketing

Performance marketing is a service of its own. Your agency can provide a separate package like this. Performance marketing is basically a term used to define online marketing and advertising strategies where you pay depending on how content performs.

For example, if you are using LinkedIn as a platform to advertise your or your client's services, you are leveraging a platform that consists of millions of potential prospects. With the help of LinkedIn ad campaigns, you are promoting ads, and the pay will depend on performance criteria such as clicks and downloads. This is where metrics come into play such as the following:

CPC (Cost Per Click): Pay based on when a user clicks on an ad.

CPL (Cost Per Lead): Pay based on when a user completes actions that qualify them as leads.

CPA (Cost Per Action): Pay based on a certain action, like completing the purchase of a product, signing up for a demo, requesting quotes, etc.

In summary, performance marketing involves a combination of advertising campaigns and online marketing services as discussed above, and this helps to provide insight to clients on how well each campaign is functioning and present results.

Website Design and Development

A company's greatest asset when it comes to marketing is its website. Undoubtedly, there will be demands from clients who will ask you to optimize their website design and content to help develop it. If you have a team of web designers and developers, you will excel in this area.

Web designing helps make the client's website accessible and comprehensible. It will also help the site to rank higher in search engine results pages (for SEO purposes). On the other hand, web developers prioritize the technical side of things, such as programming to make the website fully operational and fixing any bugs. How well a website performs can help businesses land prospective queries and convince visitors to convert into paying clients.

Graphic Design

Graphic design is another service that is in huge demand in digital marketing. For online marketing materials, you will require designs that are appealing and that communicate your brand's message.

Therefore, clients will require graphic design expertise who can support them in developing creative designs for their campaigns and also for designing content for other materials like whitepapers, posters, case studies, etc.

Market Research and Strategy

This may not sound like a traditional digital marketing service at first, but many businesses, especially startups or established corporations who are looking to release a new product or venture into a new market, will require market research services from an expert like you and your agency.

Market research helps businesses to analyze data such as specific markets, locations, competitors, business conditions, demographics, consumer buying habits, and much more. If your team has tools to conduct market research, such as online keyword research tools, content research and management software, etc., you will excel in this area.

Moreover, clients can always ask for a consultation when it comes to implementing marketing strategies for their businesses. They will look up to someone who is an expert, so if your agency has the capacity to create marketing strategies that help target the right clients, boost sales, communicate brand image, and scale their businesses, then you are providing a lot of value.

Choose a Niche for Your Agency

In the above section, you learned about several digital marketing services that you can start offering to your clients. However, a lot of options can be overwhelming, and most digital marketing agencies, when first starting out, make the common mistake of trying to be the jack-of-all-trades and provide every digital marketing service out there.

Eventually, they end up burning out, as they are unable to provide all the services they promised to their clients and end up getting bad reviews. This is a common thing I've heard from a few business owners I've met with, and our agency nearly fell into this trap early on. It was then that we realized that it was best to focus on a specific digital marketing service and be the masters of it.

Why You Need to Pick a Niche

I will tell you from experience. In most cases, a digital marketing startup that is just exploring this venture and building a client base shouldn't go all in and provide every digital marketing service they see online. Firstly, your business is still only learning from experience. You might have fewer staff who are also learning on the job and will be faced with different project deadlines. You don't want to put too much pressure on these employees when they are learning. Secondly, clients can tell when your agency is putting its heart into something. Your team may be contributing their passion and effort to delivering incredible social media marketing results for your client, but perhaps the same cannot be said for their email marketing campaigns, for instance. If you focus on a specific service, your team will be able to focus on everything and deliver quality results for clients. And lastly, clients are more likely to go to agencies that specialize in something. You have millions of prospects to choose from, but you can't please everyone.

The best strategy is to pick a section of people who are your ideal target audience and who require a particular service from your agency. This should be the service that you excel in. I'm sure you wouldn't mind getting testimonials from clients telling the world that they got the greatest service from the experts at your digital marketing agency. Check out the top companies that excel in what they do. For example, Apple is all about the iPhones, and Amazon is all about delivering consumer goods. Their brands are almost synonymous with these services and products when they come to people's minds.

In summary, you should focus on a particular niche and deliver quality service to your clients at least 90% of the time. This generates the best return on investment because you are only targeting a specific section of prospects who fit your niche, so invest your marketing initiatives into landing these clients. It is the best way to grow quickly as an agency starting out. You may think you are just starting out with zero clients and it will be difficult to find even one client if you don't offer *everything* to them, but this is a myth. If you pick a niche and become a specialist in one or two specific services, then you will find a lot of clients who will choose your agency over others who market themselves as "generalists."

How to Choose a Niche

Finding a profitable niche is the next move you have to make, and there are two steps to get you there. The first step is choosing a particular industry that you will target. As a startup, you can pick two industries if you like, but it's best to stick with one and understand the market well. The second step is to study their pain points and interests, and also analyze your agency's strengths and skills. If a particular digital marketing service is in demand and aligns with your agency's capability and capacity, then it may be the right fit for you.

For instance, we focused on SaaS businesses—especially those that provided innovative online tools for productivity or work purposes. We now had our market. Then, we analyzed their pain points and also made sure our skills aligned with their needs. We have a creative team that is good at producing and managing content. We were able to provide and focus on delivering content marketing services to our clients regularly. We also provided SEO services, but that wasn't our bread and butter. We offered it as an additional service if clients wanted them.

We didn't focus our resources or staff on PR marketing, website building, or most of the other digital marketing services you saw on the list. Eventually, we were able to generate more revenue because we consistently made our clients happy and attracted new clients through referrals. Because we specialized in a specific niche, we had a direction toward which to build a client base, and that helped our agency grow faster.

As a startup, you may wonder what markets you can target. For my agency, it took some time to sign our first few SaaS clients because it is a lucrative industry with intense competition. However, you can start small and get clients quickly by focusing on one of the profitable markets I've been studying. These include companies that do HVAC (Heating, Ventilation, and Air Conditioning), solar, plumbing, and landscaping.

You may think, why these specific sets of companies? Because these companies require a consistent pipeline of leads coming through, and these services are almost always in high demand, too. This provides an opportunity for digital marketers like you and your agency to work with them and provide services that will help them maintain a stream of incoming qualified leads.

Having said that, there are a few other profitable niches you can focus on if one fits your interests and the strengths of your agency. The energy sector has promising opportunities that can be easily overlooked by business owners, the ecommerce sector is booming, and the healthcare sector constantly needs marketing materials and campaigns running to establish their presence online. The education sector also has its opportunities, with courses, resources, and many educational programs being promoted online. Other profitable sectors include retail, fitness, and of course, SaaS.

Niching down further can provide you with additional advantages. For instance, your very specific niche could be to provide social media marketing services on LinkedIn, Facebook, and Instagram for cosmetic doctors in an area where you did in-depth research and found a market and demand for these services. This is the beauty of niching, and as a startup, this is one of the most effective methods to grow your business fast and deliver results to your clients.

Everything is learned from experience and how you scale your business. In the future, when you have built a solid client base, recruited more talented employees, and developed a large network of vendors, contractors, and freelancers, then you, as an established agency, can start providing more digital marketing services and exploring different marketplaces. In that way, you will end up diversifying your client base and multiplying your revenue over time.

Benefits of Climbing the Value Ladder

Next, you will learn a valuable concept to instill within your business mindset that will help your agency grow. It is called the "value ladder," and it is a term that describes the relationship between the brand and its customers, whereby the brand looks to keep adding more and more value for its customers. This is a concept that will scale your business, develop a high-profile client base, and lead to high-ticket sales (selling expensive products/services of high value). But everything is centered around prioritizing the relationship with the customers. Adding value is the motto of the value ladder.

You see influencers online becoming millionaires quickly nowadays. Many are becoming millionaires before even reaching their 20s. This is because they focus on providing value. For instance, you see YouTubers who focus on their niche and provide free content through their videos. They grow a big following on their social channels and then decide to take it to the next step and provide coaching and mentoring services to those who need it. Then, they look to design courses and more exclusive content to provide more and more value for their audience.

From these examples, you can see that they kept adding value and kept prioritizing their relationship with their audience to grow their following. As they climb the value ladder, the cost of their services increases along with their demand. Eventually, they can price their products/services at a high price that customers are willing to pay. This is how they increase their revenue rapidly and become millionaires.

You can follow the same strategy with your digital marketing agency startup as you aim to become an expert in your field and sell your services at high prices that match their high value.

The beauty of following a value ladder approach is that you will nurture relationships and build a growing brand image. You establish diverse revenue streams for your agency by selling both low-priced services and high-ticket services. Hence, you can serve everyone, and this is the ultimate goal that every business wants to reach.

Remember that, as a startup, you can't please everyone. When you are just starting out, you will have zero clients and little capital and resources, not to mention less experience. But once you grow as a business, have more people to delegate responsibilities to, and have more money to invest in your growth, you can eventually aim to provide your services to anyone. This is a goal that all aspiring digital marketing entrepreneurs should keep in mind.

Productized Services Boost Agency Growth

"Productized services" is a phrase used to describe services that sell like products. As you know, products can be sold easily without much hassle, and many products are in demand. They also have clearly defined pricing parameters. The benefit of productizing your services is that you can sell them to many customers and expand your income-earning potential. Hence, this is a scaling strategy that you should look to incorporate in your agency at some point. This is usually built up over a long period of time. It can take some years, but this section will give you a framework for how you can achieve this.

Simply put, productized services provide your clients with alternative packages, service agreements, and affordable options. You can sign clients and choose marketing packages that fit their budget and scope of work. You can see this being implemented all the time with many B2B companies.

For instance, you see fitness coaches online selling service packages that feel like itemized products. They have afford-able packages for clients that provide one-on-one sessions and details for how they can continue their program. Then they have packages for high-end customers who can pay more to get more time and advanced coaching sessions with the trainers.

Moreover, the process of purchasing these services is easy. They can go to the company's website and purchase the package instantly, get an automated confirmation and welcome email, and then they are contacted by the trainer immediately to plan their sessions. In a nutshell, productizing your services means making things simple and accessible.

Digital marketing services have the potential and capability to be productized. I urge you to do the same for your marketing services when it becomes feasible.

Here are the steps you can take to productize your marketing services. These steps involve many of the lessons you have already learned so far from this book:

Step 1: Pick your niche.

You already know the importance of this step, as it was discussed in-depth. You need to choose a niche that is profitable with high demand so you can focus your resources and energy on delivering results to your clients regularly.

Step 2: Determine your distribution strategy.

Next up, you need to determine how you are going to deliver or distribute your services. You might promote your content or services on social media and have prospects come to your landing page on your website to view essential service package details.

Step 3: Craft the offer.

Your agency should provide an offer that is very compelling. Good offers consist of things such as guides, courses, webinars, promotions, membership programs, loyalty programs, and much more. I advise you to keep your offers clear and straightforward; don't beat around the bush. Always list your service details properly and be transparent with what the customer can expect from you. To top it off, include a call to action in your offer (in most cases, to buy your service).

Step 4: Establish a consistent structure.

Your services need to follow a consistent structure or process that makes it easy for clients to get what they ask for. Predictability isn't a bad thing here, because good products offer consistent quality, and consumers relish that. Include features like recurring subscriptions, one-time payments, quality support, and well-written onboarding messages in your marketing service packages.

Step 5: Keep refining your services.

Remember that this process is a learning experience, and there are no limitations. As you can see, big brands are always looking to develop their products over time. You should do the same with your services by taking in feedback from customers and acting on their requests to provide more value through your services.

Eventually, after you've executed each step, you can successfully productize your services and boost your agency's revenue growth significantly.

Designing Offers That Sell Like Products

I will wrap up this chapter by providing you with a simple framework to design your service offerings in such a way that it becomes easy for you to deliver them to clients and basically make them sell like products.

Since delivering your services is the core of your business, it should be important to you that your offerings are clear. Think about it. Most sales teams fail to perform not because they are bad at selling but because they don't understand the offer clearly enough.

Prospects will become doubtful and disengage with you once they spot the flaws in your delivery or body language. For your sales team to be confident delivering the pitch, it should be tailored to the client's needs as well as convenient to follow through with.

Here are four steps to ensure you can design offers that will sell like hot products:

Develop a service that delivers the results your clients want.

In this first step, your way of thinking should be different. Think as if you are not selling the service but selling the experience; the end results. For example, if one of the client's major pain points is being unable to generate leads through emails, then your offer should focus on selling the results your client wants to see rather than on your email marketing campaigns. In this case, these desired results would include things like seeing good email open rates, getting responses, and a higher percentage of qualified leads coming in from their email copy. If you think about selling the experience and end result more than just your service, you will be able to market your service better and make more sales.

Deliver with efficiency to gain satisfaction.

The next step is to plan out how you are going to deliver your service efficiently so that you end up with a satisfied client time after time. For example, if you are designing an email marketing campaign for your client, ensure it is as efficient and high quality as possible so that you deliver the desired result and also make your client happy. For instance, you could break down your email marketing campaign into goals or milestones that will be communicated to the client with specific deadlines, project deliverables, and other details. This will not only improve workflow for your teams but also show the client a series of successes along the way to their desired end results.

Price your services reasonably.

Pricing can be a tricky procedure when you're starting out and looking to break through the competition. However, your pricing should be set in a way that makes it clear to your clients what they are paying for. Don't low-ball them with cheap prices, because this is not a good move for your agency if you want to make profits and achieve your financial goals. Instead, structure your offer in a way that makes it clear what all is involved. For example, when delivering your email marketing campaign, you can break down the pricing into smaller components. For instance, you will charge X amount per 100 emails sent, X amount for writing email copy, X amount for using the email marketing software, and so on. Or you could change your pricing strategy and adopt a revenue-sharing model. For example, you will ask for a certain percentage from the revenue they generate from your email campaigns.

Make it easy for clients to sign up for your service.

Onboarding is something that many businesses unintention-ally make rough and complicated. It doesn't need to be. Think about why products are so easy to buy. Because they are easy for people to touch, feel, and take ownership of. Once they pay the money, they instantly claim ownership of the product. Services are a different case. Once you pay the money, it may take some time to receive the service and even more time to see the full results. Hence, you need to make sure your service offer is easy for clients to sign up for. For example, once they pay for your email marketing campaign, you must instantly send them a confirmation and welcome email showing that they've purchased your service. This should also provide guidelines, links, tutorials, and other details for what their next step with you is. There are other things you can do to make sure your services are easy to sign up for, like customizing your website and landing page or implementing fewer steps to sign up.

Key Takeaways From This Chapter

- The list of digital marketing services that you can offer to your clients includes search engine optimization, paid advertising, content marketing, social media marketing, email marketing, public relations marketing, video marketing, performance marketing, web design and development, graphic design, and market research/strategy.
- Picking a niche and focusing your resources on it helps you consistently deliver quality results to your clients and boost your agency's revenue. The first step to choosing a niche is to pick a target market or industry. Then, analyze the market's pain points and interests and align your agency's strengths to deliver results.
- A value ladder is a term that describes the relationship between the brand and its customers, whereby the brand looks to keep adding more and more value for its customers. It is a mindset that will help you evolve your agency to a level you never thought possible.
- Productized services is a term used to describe services that sell like products. You can productize your services by picking a niche, determining a distribution strategy, crafting compelling offers, establishing a consistent structure, and refining your service strategy.

- Design your offer to help your services sell quickly by developing the service to meet the client's desired end result and delivering quickly and efficiently. It should also be easy to sign up for, and your prices should be reasonable.

Chapter 5

Leverage Digital Marketing Tools for Success

Take a risk and keep testing, because what works today won't work tomorrow, but what worked yesterday may work again.

— Matt Cutts

S o far, you have learned the important core concepts of digital marketing, the importance of defining and measuring goals for your agency, the strategies to target the right clients for your business, and how to align your services to deliver results consistently to those clients.

In this chapter, you will learn how you can use digital marketing tools for your agency's benefit, and this will mainly center around internal marketing. You will need to be familiar with these tools and how to use them to get customers and build a client base.

This chapter will give you an overview of digital marketing strategies you can use, as well as media outlets to target, and provide examples of marketing initiatives, such as effective email copy that is used in real-world situations, to help you deliver success and see growth for your agency.

This information and advice is derived mostly from my experience of what we used and still use in our agency, but I will also share what I've learned from other digital marketing agency owners and how they created success in their business. Let's dive straight in and learn more.

Luring Clients to Your Den: Website and Landing Page

The end goal for any business when conducting marketing online is to generate leads or conversions. This is done using their major asset—the website. The company website is the place where you invite prospects to come and convert into customers. It is your den, and your website has the power to persuade customers to buy your offer.

Leverage Your Website to Build Your Brand

It can be difficult to sell something from your business directly online; for example, on Facebook or LinkedIn. This is because a lot of competitors are snooping around looking to sign the same clients, and also because these are not the platforms where you can easily provide all the tools for your prospects to convert into customers. Hence, luring them to your website is the ultimate way to see those conversions.

Your website should be professional and should include the following:

- an appealing homepage that displays a summary of what your brand is, what you do (or your vision/goal), the products/services you offer, the clients you have (social proof), and contact information below

- an About section that explains the business's history, the management team, and your business's mission, vision, and goal
- a product/services page where you list everything in detail and its pricing (if you want to keep the pricing confidential, you can ask visitors to request for a quote)
- a page of social proof that includes the clients you have worked with, case studies, etc.
- a page that displays all the essential contact details needed for visitors to stay in touch with you, such as email address, phone number, and business address

These are the essential components that make up your professional website. Moreover, you can optimize your website by following these tips:

- Make the website mobile-friendly and responsive for mobile users.
- Include call-to-action buttons wherever necessary, like for contacting you, getting a quote, or discussing a project.
- Use simplistic designs and aim to declutter your web pages so it's easy for visitors to navigate.
- Use consistent designs that reflect your brand image and goals. For instance, you see McDonalds utilizing a consistent red and gold color theme across their website which reflects their logo and brand image. People associate with a brand better than a company.
- Ensure the content displayed on the website is more oriented toward your customers rather than making it

all about your business.

- Incorporate SEO practices to increase search engine visibility, such as including backlinks, most-searched keywords, and high-quality content.

Incorporating these practices can help you leverage your website to convert customers when they visit it. It is crucial to keep updating your website regularly to stay up to date with the latest market or online trends and also to update all necessary information related to the performance of your business. This might include things like posting recent client testimonials, case studies, new service packages, and much more.

Your Landing Page Is the Home of Sales

A landing page is a separate web page that is specifically created for marketing and sales purposes. Its ultimate goal is to urge visitors to take action, and this can include signing up for a newsletter, providing their contact information, or purchasing a product/service. Hence, it is the hub where you will include your CTA, and only conversion matters here—nothing else.

It is important not to confuse landing pages with your website's homepage because there are distinct differences between these two. For instance, your website homepage is used as a page to exhibit your business, or basically to show off. It will have many links on the page—most notably, the header that takes you to different web pages. In a nutshell, your homepage has a lot of distractions, and its goal is to educate your visitors.

However, your landing page is different. Firstly, its goal is to convert your visitors, so its design should ensure that visitors focus on specific details. You will find no links on a landing page that would take you away from the web page. The only way to move away from the landing page is either to click on the CTA button to opt-in or close the window. In a nutshell, there are very few distractions, and a visitor is put into a closed interrogation room where they can focus on the one-on-one decision to purchase your service or not.

You must know that there are two main types of landing pages that can cater to your marketing goals. One is a lead generation landing page, or lead gen page, where you collect essential information to build your lead list. This includes the prospect's name, email address, or other contact information. The other type is "clickthrough" landing pages where the end goal is to click on a CTA button that leads straight into a sales/subscription/checkout page to complete a transaction—in most cases, buying your service.

Sections of a Landing Page

It is important to know what makes a good landing page that you can use repeatedly for your business. Hence, you will need to know the major components that need to be included in one. Let's break this down for clarity:

Section #1: Primary Image, Headline, Offer, Primary CTA

This should include your company logo at the top-left corner of the page. Then, you will have an image whose main aim is to catch the user's attention and communicate a message. This is called the "hero image."

For example, if you are selling social media marketing services, then your hero image might be a person who is happy and noticing a growth in followers on their social media account. This would send a positive impression of what your landing page is communicating visually.

Then, beside the image, you can include your headline—this should spark the prospects' interest. This is followed by a brief description that states your unique value proposition. A value proposition is basically an innovative feature or service that you offer that entices the clients.

Lastly, you will include your first CTA button in this section so prospects can take action. It should be visible and clearly labeled (the CTA is the most important thing on a landing page).

Section #2: Secondary Image, Summary of Offer's Benefits

In this section, you can add a supportive image that communicates the same message as the first, and it should also be appealing. Besides that, you must include a summary of the benefits that your prospects will experience after buying your service.

You can include more supportive images here if you are illustrating different services, but the message should be to inform prospects that you can solve their pain points.

Section #3: Social Proof

Below the second section, you can insert all your social proof that shows that you have credibility and have delivered positive results in the past. This is where you can include quotes via text testimonials from satisfied clients, video testimonial clips, and logos of different brands and companies you have worked with.

Section #4: More Information, Secondary CTA

The last section of the landing page will include more space for you to add additional information such as the features of your product/service or additional videos, case studies, and much more.

This is also where you can include your secondary CTA below the additional info, and it should be center-aligned to grab the visitor's eyes once again.

The landing page ends with a footer where you display your company logo again along with other essential information such as copyrights, policy info, etc.

Optimizing the Landing Page for More Conversions

You now have the essential information for how you should craft your ideal landing page. But how well your landing page functions will depend on the content you put on it.

An appealing headline can influence prospects to stay on your page. A visually appealing image can do the same, and how well you describe the benefits of your service can help convince your prospects to buy. It is basically a sales conversation but conducted online through a web page of text and visual elements.

One practice my agency utilizes to analyze and optimize our landing page is something called A/B testing. It is a testing process where you split the landing page into two or more different versions or variations to test their effectiveness.

For example, we created two landing pages that offered the same service (social media marketing, in this case) to the same target audience. The content only varied a little between these two. We drove traffic to these two landing pages and analyzed the conversions per 1,000 visitors. We found that one of the landing pages provided a better conversion rate than the other.

Hence, we used this as a tool to learn what went right with our most successful landing page and compared it with the one that did not perform as well. We kept doing this and were able to learn how to craft the best copy, the images that worked, the social proof that was needed, and even the intricate designs that made the difference. Use the A/B testing tool to compare your landing page variations and find the best version for converting your prospects.

Despite having a good-looking, professional website or an enticing landing page, you still need visitors to land on your page. The next section will show you how you can drive traffic to your website and landing page.

The Art of Capturing and Directing Online Traffic

Generating traffic to your website or landing page is a challenge of its own. Why? Because the numbers can mislead you. Yes, there is a difference between high-quality traffic and low-quality traffic.

High-quality traffic includes visitors who fit your ideal target audience profile and whose needs align with your business offer. They are more likely to be qualified leads, and you will have a higher chance of converting them. On the other hand, low-quality traffic are just numbers, and they will wander away from your landing page, thus increasing your bounce rate.

Therefore, it is crucial to learn the avenues for capturing and directing high-quality traffic to your website. You now know about paid routes, such as using Google Ads, social media ads, sponsored content, display ads, etc., to promote your website. Paid methods are effective, but when you are starting out, it is necessary to learn the organic methods so that you can save your budget and still build success.

Generating Traffic Organically

Below, you will find many organic (free) ways to capture and direct high-quality traffic to your website or landing page. My agency has utilized these strategies and found success with them. Let's go through each of them one by one:

Quality Content

Creating content is one of the essential pillars of inbound marketing. It builds an audience and brings potential clients over to you. But you must follow an organized process to develop quality content.

For example, you start off by identifying your target audience and their interests and pain points. Then, you start conducting SEO research by using keyword research tools such as Semrush, Google Trends, and AnswerThePublic.

For any form of content—whether it is a blog post, video, podcast, or infographic—you need to write a draft or script to get all your ideas on paper. Then, you can create your content, publish it on the appropriate channels, and promote it on social media, in your email newsletters, and even on your website.

Use a content rating tool such as ContentHarmony to see if your content meets the right standards. This tool provides a good rating scale, and you can keep modifying your content —especially blog posts—to create content of higher quality.

Social Media

We will expand on social media channels in the next section, so I will be brief here. You can capture traffic organically using social media because it has the potential to make your content or posts go "viral." It is important to keep providing value on social media by answering people's questions regularly, providing more quality and helpful content, and making things interesting with intriguing posts or by conducting live Q&A sessions.

Email List

You can build an email list of your audience or potential customers by putting lead gen forms on social media or utilizing a website scraping tool to scan websites. When you get a lot of addresses, you can send out emails that provide intriguing offers or promotions that will make people want to click on them. Insert a CTA in your email that directs the recipient to your website/landing page to successfully capture traffic.

Influencer Marketing

Your company or brand can be promoted through influencers online. We did this by promoting our company using an influencer who was an expert in personal finance. We reached out in an email and asked them to promote one of our products, an analytic dashboard that measures the clicks, impressions, cost to lead, cost to conversion, and much more. In their following video, they promoted our company, and we managed to win some leads that way when potential clients became interested in our dashboard.

On-Page SEO

This was mentioned briefly in the earlier chapters, as it is part of SEO practices. It is easy to do, and all you need to do is optimize your website by adding missing elements to your web pages, such as a defined page title, header, meta description, and URL. Moreover, adding image alt-text (text to describe each image on your site) gives you more points in visibility because it makes your site more accessible to those who are using text readers.

Backlinks

Another major part of your SEO practice that has been mentioned before is including quality backlinks. The major point here is to link certain keywords or citations to external sites with high credibility and authority. For example, you might have a keyword anchor text such as "social media marketing," so you hyperlink it to another website, which is a blog about social media marketing that could be a useful resource for your readers. This helps you to establish more visibility, in the Google search engine especially. Be sure to add internal links that take visitors from one web page to another on your website (for example, include links that take you from one blog post to another blog post on your website) so they hang around your site longer.

Repurposing Content

Content repurposing is the practice of using old content and transforming it into a different form of content—ideally with improvements. For example, we took an old video talking about several ways to grow traffic organically and turned it into a blog post—this time making it more long-form and adding more updated methods. This is a good way to use old content when your team is lacking inspiration and maintain your output of quality content in all forms to drive traffic to your company website. Therefore, make use of unique topics and turn them into a video, blog post, podcast, or infographic.

Videos

Video marketing, as mentioned before, is booming. You can get your content to go viral instantly with the power of videos. Hence, this deserves a second mention, as my agency found success with producing and promoting videos, too. Make use of channels like Instagram/Facebook Stories, YouTube Shorts, and TikTok, because more and more people are watching short-form clips, which last barely 10 seconds.

Basic SEO

It is essential to prepare your website for when it pops up in the rankings of search engine results pages. For instance, voice search is now being used a lot by people because it's easier. Voice search is basically when a user uses their own voice to search a term in a search engine instead of typing it in text, like we usually do. For example, a user will say the words "What is digital marketing?" instead of typing it out. The voice recognition AI will capture the voice and make the search engine look up the search term, "What is digital marketing?" In this way, your website can pop up on Google searches when you include specific keywords in your website content. You make your content efficient for voice search by researching and including long tail keywords (at least three to five words long), including a FAQ section, and answering prospects' most common questions. Make sure your sentences in your post are brief and concise, because AI voice search tools will find smaller snippets of text more easily.

Besides the voice search, you can register your business locally on Google. Head to Google My Business and register your company name, address, contact details, and website link. When someone searches for listings of digital marketing firms in a particular location, your business may pop up in the search, and prospects can easily click on the button that directs them to your website.

Technical SEO

Again, this is a more specialized SEO practice, and you may need to bring in technical expertise. In brief, the things you and your technical team need to focus on when it comes to technical SEO include the following:

- **Page speed:** The amount of time it takes to request and load a page.
- **Crawling:** Having search engine web crawlers like bots and spiders to request and download pages from links.
- **Indexing:** Organizing information by search engines to make it search-enabled for quick responses.
- **Links:** Look to fix any broken links or redirects.
- **Meta tags:** Elements in HTML code that optimize user experience.
- **XML:** Creating XML sitemaps for subdomains. These are files that list essential website pages to make it easier for search engines to find them.

If you don't have a technical team to deal with tasks like this, you can look to hire freelancers or any business contact that specializes in technical SEO to get this job done for you.

The purpose of technical SEO is to ensure your website is optimized for a better user experience. This way, search engines such as Google can rank your website higher because they consider your optimized website of high value.

Social Media CTAs

Making it a habit to include CTA in your social media posts and content helps to drive traffic to your website. For instance, having social share buttons helps to spread your content across multiple channels. You can urge readers to keep sharing on social media. Of course, all this is made possible by going back to the first point—create quality content that adds value for your audience.

Leveraging Social Media Outlets

Social media is a powerful avenue to market your business and drive traffic to your company. Eventually, more and more people will become aware of your brand as you establish an online presence on social media.

It is essential to adopt a 70-20-10 rule when publishing content on social media. For instance, for every piece of content, 70% of it should be informational and educational for the audience, 20% should be engaging and connect with the audience emotionally, and the remaining 10% can be geared toward promotional purposes (to directly promote a service).

Many businesses make mistakes in their social media marketing strategy by making their content more than 50% promotional rather than informational. And some businesses make a mistake by creating content that is 100% informational rather than connecting with the audience emotionally and including any CTA to push for their service or product.

Paying attention to this rule will help you plan your content more effectively as you publish on social media channels. As a result, it will help you address your audience's pain points, build a positive relationship with them, make your brand more customer-centric and humanized, drive traffic to your site, and eventually, generate more leads and customers.

Now, let's explore the social media channels you can use to distribute content and find high-quality leads. Each has its benefits, so choose the ones that are right for you and start targeting potential clients right away (WordStream, 2023).

Facebook

Let's start with the king of them all—Facebook. As you probably know, it is currently home to the highest number of users. You can find a lot of Baby Boomers on this platform, as well as adults in their 20s and 30s. It is the best place to distribute informational content along with images, links, and even live videos. However, it's not the best place to grow traffic organically. Hence, you will find Facebook useful mainly for local marketing purposes, nurturing relationships on a personal level, and utilizing its paid ads.

Instagram

Instagram is home to many young adults and mostly millennials. You have better chances of developing organic reach on this platform, and you can see many influencers thriving on Instagram. It is a great platform when it comes to ecommerce, social shopping, and promoting inspiring content. You can utilize Instagram ads, too, but they are more expensive when compared to Facebook ads.

LinkedIn

In LinkedIn, you will find working professionals mostly in the age group of 40s and 50s. LinkedIn is a great place to promote long-form content and messages that communicate core values and lessons. It will be easy for you to develop organic reach with B2B companies on LinkedIn—both locally and globally. In addition to that, you can utilize LinkedIn to attract talent, potential partners, and suppliers, share company milestones, and keep in touch with industry trends.

Twitter

Twitter may have a limited reach when it comes to your audience using ads, but it is a great place to engage with customers, have discussions, and even provide some entertaining interactions. You will find a majority of users are male, in their 30s and 40s, and from the well-educated and wealthy demographics.

TikTok

TikTok is a famous tool used by influencers, as it helps to promote entertaining content in a simplified way. Even though TikTok is a platform where you find a lot of youth, businesses still manage to craft TikTok videos that can hook potential customers and generate leads. Its algorithm helps, too, when it comes to organic reach. You will find a mostly female audience on this platform, as well as teenagers. However, the nature of TikTok's platform is not ideal for building relationships with prospects, since it is more for promoting quick, entertaining clips rather than having one-on-one conversations.

YouTube

YouTube is royalty when it comes to promoting videos, and interestingly, the second largest search engine after Google. You will find the majority of users are in their mid 20s to early 40s. The best forms of content to promote on YouTube are tutorials, how-to guides, and webinars. You can leverage its SEO capability and utilize both organic and paid advertising to reach potential clients. On the flip side, making videos can be resource-heavy and time-consuming; therefore, you would need a specialized and efficient team to focus on video creation and distribute them on YouTube regularly.

With this information, you can choose which specific social media outlets align with your ideal target market, the services you provide, and the agency goals you have set. You can then develop strategies and social media goals for that platform and allocate your budget and resources accordingly for those platforms. Make use of analytics to measure and adjust your social media strategy to bring in better results.

Engaging With Emails

Let's talk about email. This is an essential skill your agency needs to have to conduct business and win clients—even if you are not providing email marketing services to clients, this is a must-have skill.

With that said, it is essential to learn to write a sales email. This format helps to hook your prospect and inject them into your sales funnel. It's mostly a cold approach, and as an agency, you should learn how to write effective sales emails to get more meetings, discovery calls, and eventually conversions.

The basic rules of an effective sales email are as follows:

- an intriguing and engaging subject line (usually a question, should be kept short)
- an introductory line or hook that entices the reader to keep reading
- body of the email should be personalized and tailored to your reader's pain points
- include specific data wherever you can, such as stats to interest the reader and catch their attention quickly
- don't talk about yourself only. Make the email more about them. Make it 80% about the reader and 20% about you.
- insert a clear CTA to urge the reader to take the next step

Utilize these tips to craft effective emails. Your typical sales email strategy should consist of a primary email followed by successive follow-up emails. Below, you will find a few primary email examples you can use that were successful for our agency's conversions. At the end, I will provide examples of follow-up emails as well.

Primary Email Examples

#1: Opening with series of questions

Subject: Do you need more leads?

Hi [First Name],

Is your business generating enough leads? Does your team have an effective strategy to generate leads consistently?

I wanted to ask because we provide lead gen solutions and have the software to find your ideal prospects' information and send automated lead gen forms and emails.

You can probably get 5x or 10x the responses by working with us in the first 6 months.

Perhaps you would be interested in a discovery call to learn more?

Regards,

[Your Name]

#2: Personalized and to the point

Subject: Did you notice this problem with your website?

Hi [First Name],

I came across your company (insert company name) from (mention source), and I felt the need to reach out.

I noticed a couple of things on your website that might be letting you down:

(Insert brief review of 2 problems you found)

I am a website designer and developer from [Your agency name], and I've worked on many website design projects. I've attached a link to one of our client's case studies if you would like to review it (insert case study link).

If you would like to sit down and have a chat about reassessing your website design strategy, I would be happy to discuss this with you.

Thank you for your time, [mention prospect's name again], and I look forward to your reply.

Regards,

[Your Name]

#3: Making the prospect think with intriguing questions

Subject: How will you acquire international clients after the latest expansion?

Hi [First Name],

I recently came across your recent post on expanding your office and services outside the US & Canada. Congratulations on this big move.

However, I'm just curious about how your sales team will devise a strategy to generate constant leads from foreign clients.

The foreign markets are different from the US & Canada regions, and they require diverse digital marketing strategies to reach your ideal clients.

We're a digital marketing agency that specializes in lead generation services across social media platforms and email campaigns. We have the software, the manpower, and the expertise to take on this mountainous task for you. So, what's stopping you?

If that sounds good to you and you might be interested, then I look forward to your reply.

Regards,

[Your Name]

#4: The magic of numbers

Subject: Does a 40% increase in leads within a month sound too good to be true?

Hi [First Name],

My name is [Your Name] from [Your Agency Name]. We utilize various digital marketing tools and channels to get companies the clients they deserve.

As our agency's unique specialty, we aim to generate a 40% increase in lead generation within 30 days. If clients don't see that exact target being met, then they receive a refund.

Does this sound like something that would work for you? If so, I would only need 10 minutes of your time to discuss what we can bring to the table for your company.

Regards,

[Your Name]

Follow-up Email Examples

#1: Following up after downloading a lead magnet

Subject: Cheers for downloading our ebook

Hi [First Name],

Thanks for downloading the [ebook name] ebook. I hope this will help you get closer to your goal of [solving the prospect's #1 major pain point].

Even when your business solves [#1 major pain point], it leads to another problem that most businesses have, and that is [introduce #2 major pain point here].

Hence, I have attached another resource on [insert additional resource name] that you will find helpful in your journey to scale your business.

If you have any questions, feel free to reply to this email, and we can schedule a one-on-one session to discuss further.

Regards,

[Your Name]

#2: Following up after a discovery call

Subject: [Your Agency]-[Client's Name/Company] follow-up

Hi [First Name],

It was a great pleasure speaking with you and discussing your [pain points/goals].

I've attached the presentation slides from our video meeting for you and your team to refer to.

If you're still curious about how we can solve your [list pain point/goal], then I would suggest we have another meeting so we can show you some numbers regarding our client's progress.

I've attached a few case studies that you may find interesting, as these clients work in the same industry as you.

If you have any questions, please do not hesitate to reach out to us. Hoping to talk soon and discuss more.

Regards,

[Your Name]

Emails help businesses stay engaged professionally with clients and prospects. Use it to your advantage and hire a team of excellent writers who can write compelling sales emails.

To become more efficient, save templates like the ones shown above and then tailor them to specific prospects. Ensuring emails are personalized is the key so your prospects won't disengage immediately, thinking that you are just a bot sending thousands of similar emails to thousands of others. Make them believe that you really want to help their business.

Implementing Your Strategies in Real-World Situations

Before wrapping up this chapter, I will provide you with three real-life situations to illustrate how you may be tasked with a digital marketing project by a client and not know where to start.

These examples are common, and we will use the most popular tools to help you tackle the first few projects.

Scenario #1: Your client wants to attract more prospects to their product landing page in only 30 days—with a limited budget.

In this situation, you need to increase the visibility of the client's product landing page. This can be done most effectively by using the Google search engine. With only 30 days and the client's limited budget, this means paid advertising is more likely to show quick results.

Head over to Google Ads and use the client's account to log in/sign up. You will find an option to switch to "Expert mode" on the homepage, so click on that to get full control of your ad campaign. Choose the option to "create a campaign without a goal guidance" and create a "Search" ad campaign. Your main goal is to get website visitors, so you can link the website or the landing page URL as the target destination whenever someone clicks on the ad.

In the next steps, you can create your campaign's name and set a start date and end date, the geographical location(s) you want to target, the target language, and even the budget. Ensure you set an end date for your campaign so that Google won't keep charging the credit card each month. Regarding the budget, you can set a daily limit; for instance, you can set it at $5 per day so Google will not spend over $150 in 30 days for the whole campaign. Google knows the best time to place the ads, too, so you don't need to worry about exceeding the specified budget.

You can then create the ad group campaigns with the specific keyword terms, and then start creating the ad by including Headline 1, Headline 2, Headline 3, and the description for the ad. You can preview your ad to see how it looks on the dashboard when you're creating the ad in real-time. Finally, you can save your changes, create more search ad campaigns, and then make them go live.

You can take this a step further by using Google Analytics to help measure the client's landing page conversions, page visits, and even your ad campaign's click-through rate. Simply head to Google Analytics and make an account using the same login information you used for Google Ads.

You will find an option called "Google Ad Links," so choose the accounts and link the respective ad campaigns to measure and run analytics. This way, you can give your client an accurate report for how the campaign is going and offer insights regarding where their visitors are coming from as well as conversion factors.

Scenario #2: Your client wants to turn website visitors into email newsletter subscribers and provide occasional automated emails.

In this situation, you will need prospects to provide email addresses and opt in for your email marketing campaigns. The best tool for beginners to use here is MailChimp.

Head over to MailChimp and create an account with your client's email and business address. Choose one of the paid plans so you can get access to the automated email feature of MailChimp. If you started with the free version, you can later upgrade to a paid plan according to your requirements.

You can start by creating a "Sign-up Form" that will pop up a few seconds after a prospect visits the client's website. You can modify the pop-up form by adding the appropriate headline, adding images, and asking visitors to enter their email addresses. You will find an option to connect a website when you make the sign-up form, so you can link the client's website.

You will be provided with HTML code, which you can simply copy/paste into the header of the client's website so it will start using the sign-up form pop-up. After that, you will already have built an email list that will be stored in your MailChimp account interface.

You can then adjust your email campaigns; for instance, you can switch from sign-up forms to welcome emails after a prospect signs up for your newsletter. You can use MailChimp's create email campaign interface to insert your subject lines, design templates, images, and much more for your automated emails. Designing an email newsletter template is as easy as designing a website. After making your email campaigns for each newsletter, you can keep track of the open rate and other insights through MailChimp's analytics dashboard.

Scenario #3: Your client wants you to generate leads for them through LinkedIn specifically—with a limited budget.

In this case, your client's company wants to get leads through LinkedIn. The best tool to use here is the LinkedIn lead gen forms.

Log in to your client's LinkedIn Business account and head over to the Advertise section. You will find an ad manager dashboard, and you can start setting up a new ad campaign group and then ad campaigns.

You can create ads in formats such as Sponsored InMail ads or Sponsored Content ads that will be displayed on the target audience's LinkedIn feeds. Choose either based on the client's product/services, and set the target audience based on LinkedIn's detailed filters.

You can customize your ad formats further by choosing single image ads, carousel ads, video ads, or message ads. You can then set a start and end date for your campaign and also specify the daily budget (similar to Google Ads). You can then create pre-filled forms for when the target audience clicks on the ad, so it will take them to a form where they can fill in essential contact details.

You can also place LinkedIn lead gen forms on the client's LinkedIn company page by heading to the page in admin view and setting up the lead gen form using the analytics dashboard. You can set up a small banner on the company profile page that provides a CTA for page visitors to click and provide contact details for leads.

Online Resources to Help With Your Digital Marketing Journey

Our agency was able to learn these methods and complete our campaigns successfully for our digital marketing projects using many helpful resources on the job. Even without prior experience, we utilized online resources that offered simple tutorials and digital marketing knowledge that made us into the experts we are today. We applied our knowledge to client projects and were able to get better at it one project at a time.

Bookmark the following resources on your browser, and always refer to them when you encounter any challenges down the line. The online resources that helped me and my agency include the following:

- **Google Ads Blog**

As the name suggests, this blog is tailor-made for Google Ads. If you want to learn more about Google Ads, then this is the blog to go to. It also contains a wider variety of digital marketing-related topics associated with Google. Moreover, you can head to Google's Skillshop and enroll in free certification courses. Their modules are simple and insightful, teaching you how to use Google Ads and other online advertising tactics with ease. This is a great way to develop your skills quickly.

- **Google Analytics Academy**

As you know, analytics is an essential aspect of one's digital marketing strategy. Google Analytics is the boss of digital analytics dashboards; hence, this blog is dedicated to teaching you how to use Google Analytics and its tools. It is so beginner-friendly that anyone without prior knowledge can benefit from this blog.

- **Ahrefs**

Ahrefs is an effective SEO tool, and it is also an insightful blog where you can learn more about various SEO techniques and tricks, such as carrying out effective keyword research, building links on your website for better outreach, and much more.

- **HubSpot**

HubSpot needs no introduction, as it is one of the most popular digital marketing tools. What makes them stand out is their amazing and detailed blog. I mean, if you want thorough guides and specific steps, then this blog is your go-to place to master digital marketing practices. It also has a sister blog, HubSpot Academy, which provides free certifications. Here, you can develop your digital marketing skills quickly.

- **WordStream**

WordStream is a popular online advertising management tool. As you can see, these are all digital marketing tools, and they provide the best learning resources. WordStream provides content on search marketing and helps you to understand how to strategize your advertising campaigns properly as a local niche business owner.

- **Neil Patel**

Neil Patel is a well-known digital marketer, and his blog also provides insightful content that touches upon various forms of digital marketing with detailed step-by-step video tutorials.

This is also another great place for beginners without any prior knowledge of digital marketing.

- **Social Media Examiner**

Social Media Examiner is a great resource if your niche is focused on social media marketing. It provides insightful content on how to bolster your online marketing game across different social media platforms, including Facebook, LinkedIn, Instagram, and Twitter. This is also another useful resource I refer to for well-explained beginner tutorials.

- **Moz**

Moz is widely associated with SEO-related content, and this can be valuable if your niche is focused on that. You can refer to the Moz SEO Learning Center to learn more about various SEO practices and other digital marketing techniques.

- **Backlinko**

Backlinko is another great resource when it comes to learning about basic SEO practices and gaining a lot of insightful knowledge. It provides detailed instructional guides on advanced link-building techniques, as well as various other blog content.

- **Unbounce**

Unbounce is a great tool for building simple landing page designs for marketing purposes. Beginners like it because of its simple drag-and-drop feature. Moreover, the Unbounce Blog provides insightful content on how to increase conversion rates through landing pages, tips for optimizing your landing pages, and much more. You will also find this blog very helpful.

Key Takeaways From This Chapter

- Your website and landing page are the hubs to generate leads and sales. Building an effective website and landing page helps to improve conversion rates.
- You can capture and direct online traffic to your website/landing page organically by developing quality content and using SEO practices, social media, email marketing, influencer marketing, and video marketing.
- You can also generate online traffic easily through paid advertising, such as Google Ads or social media ads.
- The major social media channels to target prospects are Facebook, Instagram, LinkedIn, Twitter, TikTok, and YouTube. Utilize the 70-20-10 content rule when promoting content on social media channels.
- Writing effective primary and follow-up emails help to engage with prospects, understand them better, and convert them into customers.
- Refer to online resources and keep learning on the job. Use your knowledge and apply it practically to client projects to improve your skills one contract at a time.

Chapter 6

Retain and Build a Client Base

Do what you do so well that they will want to see it again and bring their friends.

— Walt Disney

After your agency has settled in and started acquiring customers, your goal is to build a large client base. However, there is an art to retaining your existing clients rather than just acquiring new ones.

When you retain your current clients, they keep providing you with repeat business and increase your revenue by a significant percentage for years. It can be expensive for an agency to acquire a new client, but cost-effective to retain an existing one and keep getting business from them.

This chapter will take you through effective retention strategies that you can implement in your agency so that you can focus on making your existing clients happy as you start building a solid client base. Execute these strategies well, and

Richard Hedberg

you'll never have to worry about them leaving you for a competitor.

The Importance of Relationship Marketing

For any business, client retention is crucial. If you want to make six or seven figures for your digital marketing business, you need to retain clients for years. In a typical digital marketing business scenario, clients get excited to work with you and are involved with what you are doing for the first two months. Then after three or four months, they will start doubting their decision to sign with you if they aren't seeing results; then they will begin to think about their perceived return on investment with you.

But there are other reasons why clients may leave you other than not bringing in good results. You may be bringing them decent results, but that doesn't mean you've solidified the relationship. They might still leave you based on other reasons. The most common reason is not getting the experience they wanted and not feeling heard or paid attention to. This may sound like I'm talking about a typical real-life romance story, but it's also true in the business world.

To address this factor, the first step you need to take is to measure your customer retention rate by using a metric to identify the key challenges in your business; you will also need to identify the number of new clients you want to target each month to offset the clients who are leaving.

You can measure customer retention rate, or CRR, by using the following formula:

CRR = ((E-N)/S)x 100

112

S = Clients you have at the start

E = Clients you have at the end

N = Clients acquired during that specific time period

So, let's say you start the quarter of a new financial year with 30 clients, and during that period, you end up acquiring 25 clients but losing 5 of them. At the end of the quarter, you end up with 50 clients.

So, your CRR here is calculated this way:

(50-25)/30 x 100 = 83%

This is your client retention rate in this example.

Most digital marketing agencies should aim for above 80%, and if you can do that, you are doing a pretty good job. Of course, a perfect 100% is a rare thing to see because in any business, you are likely to lose at least one client even if you are doing everything right. You can't please everyone, and there could be any reason why that one client will leave you.

If you make 8/10 or 9/10 of your clients happy and they stay with you, you are not the one to blame. But if your percentage goes below the 80% mark, it shows that you need to work on your customer retention strategies. So, how do you go about this?

There is a term called relationship marketing, which is basically a marketing strategy that focuses on developing meaningful relationships with clients so that you achieve long-term client satisfaction and brand loyalty.

My agency uses this strategy to retain our existing clients so that we don't need to break a sweat finding new ones, and we usually rely on our inbound leads to get new clients. This is due to the success of our promoting content online and other inbound marketing tactics.

Having long-term clients helps to boost your agency revenue because satisfied clients means happy clients. They keep coming to you for more projects when their business keeps doing well. That means they will come to you for high-value marketing initiatives—with bigger budgets—and they'll accept higher prices from you because they trust your expertise.

Loyal customers also do a fine job of referring other clients to you—which brings in even more revenue. Furthermore, loyal clients are an opportunity for you to do cross-selling or up-selling for your digital marketing services.

For example, up-selling means your client may require social media marketing on LinkedIn, but you up-sell by offering them an entire social media marketing package for all platforms.

On the other hand, an example of cross-selling might be when your client requires social media marketing on LinkedIn, but you also offer them email marketing services so that they get better responses from prospects.

To build an effective relationship marketing strategy, you need to focus on the following pillars:

- personalized customer service (make it all about them)
- constant customer engagement (wherever they are, always engage with them)
- customer loyalty rewards (offer incentives or discounts whenever necessary)

- create content that touches the heart (promote compelling brand stories)
- seek their feedback (ask for feedback from customers frequently)
- integrate technology for efficiency (use latest tech to always deliver quality work)

By focusing on the above pillars, you can strategize your marketing efforts effectively to establish loyalty with your customers.

I will share in the next sections a few things that helped us retain our digital marketing clients more often, and I recommend you incorporate these in your business, too.

Getting Things Off to a Great Start: Nail Your Onboarding Process

The biggest mistake many digital marketing agencies make is sealing the deal and forgetting to set up an effective welcoming or onboarding process for their new clients. In many cases, they celebrate the achievement of finalizing a deal and signing a client but then completely forget about them later. Once a client signs up, they can quickly pick up on vibes that may tell them this was a mistake if you don't have an effective onboarding process that creates that positive first impression and reassures the client that they made a good decision in signing up with you.

Therefore, you need to implement these strategies in your onboarding process, just like my agency does, and this will provide you with positive results that enhance the customer experience with your agency.

Step 1: Send a welcome kit.

After a digital marketing client signs with you, I know you'll be excited to celebrate closing a deal, but the first thing you must do is send them a welcome kit.

This can be done by sending them a welcome email with a good greeting card-type of design that thanks them for the trust they have put in your agency. You can send them a summary of the quote, the pain points they want to solve, the solutions you have proposed, and the desired outcome you have promised.

In a nutshell, your goal is to implement a welcome message that goes something like this:

Welcome to XYZ Agency!

Thank you for choosing us. We are delighted to partner with you. I am your digital marketing Account Manager, and I will be here to assist you with anything you need. Please watch our welcome video that will take you through what we will work on [or any tutorials they will need to work on a platform you have designed]. Here is a list of team members who will assist you in specific departments.

This example message provides transparency and encourages clients to get excited that they made the right choice with you. Also, there are some agencies that take this further and send a tangible welcome kit through the mail. We started doing this as well halfway through our first year, and this included sending them physical greeting cards, our in-house designed digital marketing mini guide, and other freebies.

Yes, this is going to cost you some money, but I have noticed that it's those small things that you do for your clients that make them stay with you longer and think twice about considering competitors.

Step 2: Integrate each other's digital worlds.

The next step is to ensure both parties (your agency and the client) have effective communication lines established for the duration of your business relationship.

For example, this is where you ask for your client's accounts, tools, and other dashboards that may be useful for the digital marketing project. Hence, you will be exchanging passwords and other confidential information during this phase, so ensure you have a non-disclosure agreement (NDA) prepped and signed by both parties to make sure no confidential data will be leaked or misused by either party.

You can also discuss the communication channels you both will be using for seamless collaboration. It might be communicating through Slack, email, or other social media platforms. Be sure you provide accurate availability so that both parties respect each other's boundaries. If a representative of an agency says they're always available, then that is considered overpromising, and that can lead to client dissatisfaction.

Step 3: Schedule a kickoff meeting.

The next step is to schedule a kickoff meeting for the project. This is an integral part to help your client familiarize themself with your agency's work process and understand more about how you and your agency will work toward achieving their marketing goals.

You can make this meeting informal in nature, as it proves to be a good way to relax some nerves and allow everyone to be in a good mood to start building a healthy business relationship.

It's All in the Details: Know Your Client Well

Another important factor that determines the health of a relationship between a client and a digital marketing agency is how well they know each other. Remember that your client is entrusting you with their business and giving you access to their marketing channels.

They are giving you the authority to boost revenue for them. Hence, for this to work out perfectly, you must gather as much information as you can about your client. Only then can you deliver the best service possible.

Gather Information That Helps You Understand Clients Better

Gathering information should start as early as when you send a proposal to your prospect. After that point, you should continue with constant meetings to understand more of their pain points, review each stage in the project, and update them on your progress; you should learn something new each day about them.

The type of information you should be looking to gather includes the products and services they offer, their target audience and buying habits, analysis of their top competitors, goals, and major challenges.

Moreover, you should learn about the marketing strategies that they may have used in the past, what may or may not have worked, and all the software/technology they are using. Eventually, you need to learn about their budget and financial goals, and you should allocate their budget wisely toward the marketing campaigns.

Some agencies take this further by acquiring soft information, such as knowing the company's dreams, their attitude in business, their expectations, what they believe differentiates them from their competitors, their interests/hobbies, etc. This can be done by hosting informal talks, and you can establish a good relationship with your clients this way.

Assemble all this information into a document where you store all client information. Once you've done your research and understand your client, you can use this as a template to carry out the project initiatives effectively. Moreover, showing an investment in your client will show that you are invested in the relationship and in delivering the best results they can expect.

Establish Your Communication Roadmap

Another important thing you need to focus on is communication with your client. One of the most common reasons why clients end up leaving agencies, despite decent results, is because they are not being paid attention to, not feeling heard, or feeling isolated. If you are going to treat your client as a partner, you need to be more involved with them.

One fine way we do this is by meeting monthly to discuss the progress we are making and how they're growing as a business. We provide insights through analytics, graphs, and other data presentations, and trust me, most clients get excited about this.

Let's compare two agencies as examples. They both provide the same service to the same client. Agency 1 hasn't communicated much with the client or updated them regarding their progress for three months, and they are barely achieving growth. On the other hand, Agency 2 communicates regularly and provides progress reports and data to check in frequently. In this example, both of these agencies are barely achieving growth.

But the most interesting part is, the client is going to have more patience with Agency 2 and most likely ditch Agency 1 after those three months. This is because Agency 2 communicates more often and shows the client something that they can keep track of, giving them a reason to stick with it. So, if you are an agency who can produce results and also communicate regularly with your clients by providing updated intel and reports, you are much more likely to keep your clients for more than two years, at least.

Hence, the lesson here is that you have to earn a good relationship through doing these small things that matter to the client and showing them that you are heavily invested in them and their business.

Treat Your Digital Marketing Clients Like Partners

It is essential to treat your clients not as customers but as partners. After all, an agency-client relationship is about taking their business to the next level by boosting their marketing results and achieving their ultimate goal—to increase revenue.

So, what can you do to be more like a business partner rather than a supplier for these clients?

Proactiveness Is the Key to Impressing Clients

Being proactive is one of the key ways to establish a strong client relationship and strengthen client loyalty. When your agency can be more proactive rather than reactive with your clients, you establish authority and credibility in the field. Letting your client know what your next move will be makes you look like a visionary in front of them. It inspires your clients to stick with you and get excited about a long-lasting working relationship, with many projects to come.

For example, always make the first move and suggest new marketing campaign ideas and strategies that will take your clients' results to the next level. Even if it is an up-selling or cross-selling tactic, clients will appreciate that you care about making their business successful and will trust your expertise in delivering results for them.

Instead of waiting for them to ask you to start a new campaign with their idea, you should propose ideas to them first. Moreover, you should always keep them in the loop. That's another proactive move. For example, warn them in advance about any changes in a particular platform, legal steps, or anything else that may jeopardize your ongoing project with them.

Remember that clients sign up with your agency based on services that were previously defined and that you promised to deliver. Now, what distinguishes good agencies from the best ones is that good agencies execute services based on what was agreed upon with the client, and then they call it a day. On the other hand, the best agencies execute those agreed upon services but also go above and beyond by planning future projects for their clients. If your clients see you as the visionary, they will believe they signed a gem and will keep you for many years.

Plan initiatives and future projects that your client may benefit from in the next quarter, such as

- solving more challenges you have identified in their business.
- devising marketing strategies to combat seasonal changes.
- optimized marketing strategies to increase sales beyond their target.
- offering additional services that will solve other specific challenges they're facing.

Clients will love this, and they will see that you care for their business. This makes them see you as a business partner.

Be a Mentor to Your Clients

On top of that, keep educating your client and teaching them something new. A good thing to do is to break down your digital marketing process and help them understand each move your team will make to lead to success of the campaigns. Clients love transparency, and also, it is valuable to teach them things they don't know.

One thing my agency does with our clients is scheduling a review phase every three or four months. This is a long meeting where we meet to discuss the progress of the project, as well as the client's business in general.

This helps us understand the customer's concerns during an ongoing project, and it also keeps both parties involved throughout the working relationship.

Key Takeaways From This Chapter

- Customer retention is crucial for any business, not just marketing agencies. To measure your customer retention rate, use the following formula: CRR = ((E-N)/S)x 100

- Relationship marketing is a marketing strategy that develops meaningful relationships with clients that lead to long-term client satisfaction and brand loyalty.

- To build an effective relationship marketing strategy, focus on making your customer service personalized; provide constant customer engagement, loyalty rewards, and valuable content; keep asking for their feedback; and integrate technology for work efficiency on client projects.

- Establish a solid onboarding process so that clients know they've made the right decision in signing with your agency. For instance, send a welcome kit, integrate each other's digital worlds, and schedule a kickoff meeting.

- Gather important information about your client's business in general, including their core interests, so that you understand them well and can align your strategies to deliver the most success for them.

- Build a communication roadmap to keep your clients updated with reports and insights on ongoing projects.

- Treat your clients like partners. Being proactive helps you to stand out against other agencies and encourage loyalty from your clients.

Chapter 7

Scale and Automate Your Agency

You don't build a business, you build people, then people build the business.

— Zig Ziglar

This final chapter will walk you through strategies and tips for how digital marketing agencies in real life scale and automate their business. This is essential for ultimate success, if you want to end up earning up to 7 or 8 figures in revenue annually.

When running a business, it is crucial to have a growth mindset to make it grow. This helps with not only making more money as a company but also surviving in a dynamic market, where new challenges and competitions pop up out of the blue. Most businesses fail because they fail to adapt, and this is due to a failure to scale and grow.

In this chapter, you will learn how to be more efficient as a digital marketing agency by learning a few key scaling strategies.

Personally, we have opted for a couple of these strategies, and others are inspired by other agency owners. These are all real-world strategies, and all are effective if you can commit to them.

In addition, at the end of the chapter, you will learn about all the digital tools your agency can use to deliver maximum value to your customers and boost your organization's work efficiency.

Scalable Strategies for Your Agency: Dominate the Digital Marketing World

Let's go through four scaling strategies that you can implement as you start building a client base and aim to take your agency growth to the next level.

These methods will help you save money and also maximize your agency's revenue potential.

This is how agencies scale and outperform in such a short time—they utilize scaling strategies or models and stick to them.

Scaling Strategy #1: The Sales Funnel Model (Default)

The sales funnel model—or should I say, the default business process—is what most agencies follow. For example, the process goes like this. You start advertising on social media and search engines with Google Ads, Facebook Ads, LinkedIn Ads, and so on. Then, you generate leads by acquiring prospects for your sales funnel by taking them to a sales page—which can be your typical landing page or opt-in forms. Some agencies find success with using video sales letters (VSLs), which explain their services, show various case studies and testimonials, and convince prospects to sign a contract.

This is your typical model, as we've touched on throughout this book. Now, you can keep utilizing this model to generate more leads and get more clients interested in signing with you.

In this step, it is important to delegate duties and have a team that can be on their toes to keep that pipeline flowing, with new leads coming through all the time. However, you can take things to the next level by considering the other scaling strategies that I'm going to explain next.

Scaling Strategy #2: The Outsourcing Model

The next scaling strategy I want to present is the outsourcing model. Fundamentally, as an agency grows, you'll need to scale it by delegating duties to others. Eventually, you will need some helping hands. This usually comes in the form of hiring staff. The outsourcing model suggests that you can outsource your tasks to outside people, such as suppliers, vendors, freelancers, and contractors.

When a big contract, such as a client requiring social media marketing services, is acquired, you will outsource duties to freelancers or contractors who are specialized in social media marketing, graphic design, paid ad management, and so on. This helps you to save money when it comes to managing staff, but this model also requires a large network of people, so you need to have a strong communications system and established workflow to be sure you have the right people available in advance when assigning projects.

Of course, the people who will manage these projects will partly come from your own staff, but most of the technical work will be outsourced to digital marketers and other experts outside of your agency. Many agencies do this, as it is much more cost effective to pay contractors or freelancers on a per-project basis than pay an employee on an hourly basis.

Scaling Strategy #3: The Webinar Model

The next scaling strategy involves introducing a marketing initiative into your default sales funnel, which was discussed in scaling strategy #1, in the form of a webinar. For example, your default sales funnel starts off by running paid ads on platforms to lead prospects to an opt-in form or landing page, right? But in this strategy, you are going to lead them to a webinar—hosted by your agency.

Webinars are a great way to generate thousands of leads through hosting a video conference for only two or three hours. In these webinars, you provide value to your audience by educating them on various aspects of digital marketing and introducing solutions to their pain points. Your content team can do a fine job in developing ideas for webinars.

You will charge a small fee for each sign-up for these webinars, and nowadays, lots of people will pay for them because they are more and more interested in getting educated by experts. These webinars act as a way to offset your paid ads expenditures through acquiring sign-up fees for access.

So, as you can see, your agency can neutralize the costs of running paid ads by offering webinars, and you will also generate qualified leads by the time people finish watching them. Moreover, you will see better conversion rates because you've established authority through these webinars.

Of course, this strategy requires a content team that is ready to provide great ideas for a good workshop or webinar, and you should have people participate who have great presentation skills. This scaling strategy is a popular one for many digital marketing agencies these days, and for good reason.

Scaling Strategy #4: The SaaS Subscription Model

The last scaling strategy is something inspired by my time working with SaaS businesses. Their business model inspired me to see that if our agency can make our own marketing process systems and software and offer them to our clients as a subscription, then not only will it automate our work process, it will maximize our revenue potential.

This is being practiced by many digital marketing agencies who have a team of software developers, and they offer their digital marketing software, such as CRMs, landing page creation software, or ad campaign manager, in exchange for a subscription fee model, so they earn a fee every month.

However, this is the ultimate scaling step, and if you need to pull this off, you need to be super committed to your agency and have a technical team at your disposal to assist with developing the software and provide support for clients when they use your digital marketing software.

Moreover, this scaling strategy may only be feasible later on when your agency has grown in money and available resources. At that point, you may consider taking the big step and shifting your business model into a SaaS-based subscription model.

Build an Agency That Is Ready for Maximum Growth Potential

The above scaling strategies provide a framework for growing as an agency. However, there is a lot more you can do to scale your agency to greater heights.

Here are a few more tips from my experience as a successful agency owner, as well as insights from other successful agency owners with whom I've sat down and talked. We narrowed them down to the following points.

Build a Team That Fits Your Agency's Culture.

As an agency, you must define your core values to determine your organizational culture. These can include anywhere between three and five core values. For example, your agency's cultural values might be hiring people with integrity, teamwork, a growth-mindset, compassion, and loyalty.

Then, you can orient your recruiting or hiring team to find talent that matches these core values so you will build a team of those who exhibit these traits. This way, you will have people in your agency who understand the agency's culture and can avoid bringing in people who don't exhibit these traits.

Therefore, this means that your recruiting process shouldn't hire in a rush. You must take the time to vet candidates and choose the right talent for your agency. Don't worry if it takes a lot of time; just don't regret making the wrong hiring decisions.

Learn to Say "No" to Clients Who Bring You Down.

Remember how I said earlier in the book that you can't please everyone? This applies when scaling your agency to the next level as well. Despite targeting the right clients for your business, you will have some clients whose working relationship can be toxic, and these clients just won't hear you out or buy into the suggestions you offer.

These types of clients are better left alone, as they will only drain your time and create havoc in your agency over the long term. Eventually, paying too much time on them can lead to ruining relationships with other clients with whom you have formed a solid relationship already.

It is better to say no to such clients who won't hear you out and focus on the clients who have put their faith in your services and have the positive attitude to form a healthy business relationship. Because, as we now know, we don't treat our clients as customers but as partners.

Be Strict With Getting Your Payments.

This is an important mindset that you should adopt if you want to scale your agency. Sometimes, clients can take you for granted and offer silly excuses to delay payments, and this can significantly affect your agency's cash flow. After all, you've got debts, office rent, and salaries to pay for.

If a client doesn't pay you on time once, it doesn't bode well for getting on-time payments from them in the future, which can lead to huge problems. Hence, the best strategy is to always ask for payment upfront and be *strict* about it. You are not here to play games with them. Set your boundaries and establish some authority over this.

When you receive payments upfront and on time, you ensure there is positive cash flow in your agency, and this helps you in the long run to scale your agency quickly. We did this at my agency, and it was an absolute game-changer for our financial resources.

Work With Clients Who Have Bigger Budgets.

This is another simple tactic to avoid agency burnout, and it solely depends on how much staff and resources you have. If you have fewer employees, for instance, it will be best to keep working with fewer clients who have bigger budgets instead of working with lots of clients with smaller budgets. This can cause you and your agency to become completely burned out.

Eventually, you might not even enjoy doing digital marketing anymore, and this is certainly something we want to avoid. Hence, make it a strategic approach to work with clients who have bigger budgets so that you can not only focus on these few clients but also see better cash flow to scale quickly.

Build a Team of Leaders.

It is important that you don't fall into the trap of running everything on your own. This is one mistake I made early on because I had a "control freak" nature, but when I learned that a few of my employees exhibited leadership traits, it helped me be more calm and hopeful for my agency's future. I trusted them with many responsibilities and delegated duties.

This is the first and most important step for you to set your agency up for automation. Find good leaders in your organization and nurture them as soon as possible. When you work alongside them, you will find things are easier and enjoyable for you as an entrepreneur in the long run. Moreover, this helps you to scale your agency and take it to another level.

Celebrate Each Milestone With Your Team to Boost Morale.

It is essential to keep the positive vibes going in your agency, and this can be a tough thing to do consistently for years on end. Hence, a simple and effective tactic is to celebrate small wins whenever they come up.

Our small wins included: completing each client project, completing 10, 50, then 100 projects, yearly milestones, and the list goes on. When you celebrate these small victories, it provides motivation for your team to keep going and aim for more achievements. This brings your organization together as a community.

This is crucial even if you're bringing new employees in, as you'll want them to integrate and get along with your veterans.

Keep Adapting.

Digital marketing is a market that is always changing. You will find new things popping up and old things that you used to depend on becoming obsolete. It is your job to identify these trends and keep up with this ever-changing market. Keep adapting, and your agency will stay on top.

Scaling Your Organizational Structure and Hiring More People

Let's talk about scaling. This involves mapping out your organization's structural chart and getting people who can fill in those essential roles. Even if you decide to outsource most of your campaigns, it is still important to have employees in your agency who can run the show for you.

This is part of the automation process as a digital marketing entrepreneur.

When scaling into a larger agency, generally speaking, there are two major types of organizational communication structures—centralized and decentralized. Centralized communication is led by one senior person, where all formal decisions go through them and then across to all departments beneath them. For example, if your agency follows a centralized organizational structure, it means you are the only person who can make formal decisions, as you are the CEO, and this will be communicated across all the departmental heads and staff beneath you. The downside to this is that when you scale to a large organization, everyone beneath you will always be waiting for your formal decisions to address any and all challenges and issues.

Therefore, for larger agencies, a decentralized communication structure works best. This means that you will be delegating responsibility to departmental heads or other senior managers beneath you, and they will have the power to make formal decisions concerning those departments. Following a decentralized communication structure helps you to combine intellectual minds, and this makes scaling easier when you fill those roles with people who fit your company culture. This is why building a team of reliable leaders is crucial.

If your agency decides to scale globally, then a geographical organization structure will be necessary. This means you can follow a decentralized organizational structure just as you do locally but across regions. For example, you will have separate senior heads responsible for each region, such as Asia, North America, Europe, Middle East and North Africa, Oceania, etc.

Here is an example of a digital marketing agency team structure that you can follow. This helps you to address all your essential needs and find the right talent suited for each role.

Director of Digital Marketing: Responsible for leading and strategizing all digital marketing activities.

Digital Marketing Manager: Responsible for day-to-day managing and executing all digital marketing campaigns through in-house or external agencies.

Digital Marketing Account Manager: Liaising between the client and the digital marketing team to ensure all projects go smoothly. Can act as a consultant or a project manager.

SEO Manager: Manages and monitors SEO-related campaigns and has a team of specialists working under them.

Content Marketing Manager: Strategizes and manages the overall content marketing strategy and campaigns internally, and also for clients. Has a team of specialists working under them.

Performance Marketing Manager: Manages performance marketing campaigns that drive sales to the agency. Has a team of specialists working under them.

Ad Manager: Manages and oversees daily digital ad campaigns through platforms internally and for clients.

Social Media Manager: Strategizes and manages social media marketing and other activities for the business. Has a team of specialists working under them.

Email Campaign Manager: Strategizes and implements email marketing automation workflow and campaigns. Has a team of specialists working under them.

Analyst: Responsible for analyzing and reporting the performance of all digital marketing campaigns and channels. This is crucial for campaign managers and specialists to know in order to be more effective with their campaigns.

Media Planner: Responsible for planning digital ad campaign channels, allocating budget, and tracking the performance of all paid media initiatives.

Copywriter: A specialist in writing sales copy, blog content, and other written marketing copy. Can have a team of associate copywriters working under them.

Graphic Designer: Responsible for creative designs for digital marketing campaigns and for other marketing and business initiatives.

Web Designer and Developer: Acts as the development team for designing website user interfaces and also other development concerns required by the business.

Of course, other general business departmental heads should be present as well, such as the following:

HR Manager: Responsible for recruiting talent and maintaining employee records.

Financial Manager: Responsible for strategizing and managing financial business goals.

Marketing Manager: Responsible for strategizing and overseeing marketing strategies and initiatives for the business.

Sales Manager: Responsible for leading the sales team to increase conversions and acquire clients.

IT Manager: Responsible for overseeing day-to-day IT-related tasks in the agency.

Hiring Talent to Fill Essential Roles

For choosing the right talent, and also increasing your chances of acquiring employees, follow these steps and integrate them into your hiring process. This helped our agency a lot to acquire talented employees, and we also made plans to fill significant roles to scale our agency and keep the workflow running smoothly.

Keep Expanding Your Outreach.

This is an essential step because most hiring managers put their eggs into one basket and recruit candidates from only one source. You need to be more diverse and have your hiring team expand their reach to find talented candidates from various sources. This includes social media platforms such as LinkedIn, Facebook, and various job portals such as Indeed, Glassdoor, etc. Moreover, making use of networking events and academic programs can help you find talented people who also fit into your company culture well.

Know What Skills You Are Looking for.

Doing research on what skills each role requires helps you find the ideal candidate you are looking for. For example, let's say you want to hire someone for a digital media planner position in your agency, but you don't know exactly what skills they require. You are only one Google search away from knowing exactly what skills a specific role or position requires, and these are skills based on the current market standards. This helps you to know how to write your job description clearly and also ensures you hire the right candidates who exhibit those skills.

Make Succession Plans Wherever Necessary.

This is a long-term thinking strategy, but it involves identifying the agency's top performers and preparing them to take on more significant higher roles. This helps you to not only save on the costs of recruiting but also keep some of your top performers in the agency loyal and happy. Moreover, you should save data on your previous qualified candidate profiles who didn't get the position. Most agencies maintain a huge pipeline of qualified candidates and talent so they can refer back to them and reach out to them when a new position opens up.

Market Your Agency as the Place to Work.

Brand recognition is crucial, because when employees dream about working at their dream company, they don't dream of startups. They dream of working for established and globally known brands and companies such as Google, Microsoft, and Apple. Hence, you will need to market your company in a way that it is seen as *the* place to work. For example, you can include video testimonials of your employees saying positive things about your workplace. This will help motivate candidates to apply with your agency. Moreover, you can encourage employee referrals in your agency so that you have more luck hiring talented candidates through your own employees' words and effort.

List of Tools for Scaling Your Digital Marketing Agency

We will wrap up this chapter by giving you a list of tools that you can use when you're running a digital marketing agency. In an agency, efficiency is important, especially when dealing with a large volume of client projects.

Hence, I will break down the digital tools that you can use for each department to boost your workflow.

Tools for Content Creation

These tools can help you with content ideas, keyword research, and target audience requirements. They can improve your team's efficiency when it comes to content creation for client projects.

- Google Trends
- Semrush (Topic research)
- SpyFu
- SE Ranking
- Clearscope
- Curata

Tools for Social Media Marketing

These tools can help your team to manage your social media marketing content plans and track everything when handling social media accounts for your clients.

- Hootsuite
- Iconosquare
- PromoRepublic
- Sendible
- CoSchedule
- Agora pulse
- Buffer
- Sprout Social

Tools for Email Marketing

These tools can help your team with automated email marketing campaigns and provide you with fine reporting dashboards to improve workflow and make your email marketing cost-effective.

- Mailchimp
- ActiveCampaign
- Sender
- Brevo
- Drip
- Klaviyo

Tools for Automating Digital Marketing Workflow

These tools can help your team in general to streamline work processes, such as inbound marketing, outbound marketing, sales analysis, ROI, tracking, and analytics.

- Whatagraph
- Zapier
- Act-On
- AgencyAnalytics

Tools for Optimizing Conversions

These tools can help your team with generating leads and improving conversion rates for clients. These include landing pages, tracking website visits, and providing analytics on leads and conversion rates.

- Unbounce (great for creating landing pages)
- WhatConverts
- Mailshake
- Albacross

Tools for CRM (Customer Relationship Management)

These tools are utilized for managing a list of prospects or clients when reaching out to them and can help to build long-term business relationships by storing important data, scheduling meetings, and much more.

- Hunter
- Salesforce
- HubSpot
- Usersnap (good for collecting customer feedback)
- Right Inbox
- Calendly
- Keap
- Chargebee

Tools for Project Management

These tools help when it comes to enhanced collaboration and improved workflow when managing different projects.

- Asana
- Trello
- Slack
- Teamwork
- Mosaic
- Monday.com
- Scoro

Tools for Video Conferencing and Live Webchat

These tools can help to communicate with clients and others in your team, as video conferencing tools are the most popular avenue when working remotely and reaching out to clients outside your region.

- Zoom
- Google Duo
- Skype
- MobileMonkey (Integrate mobile messages with chatbots)

Tools for Graphic Design

These tools can help your team of designers and marketers to develop designs for content, prototyping, and increasing their workflow.

- Canva
- Adobe (XD, Photoshop, or Express)
- Placeit
- 99designs
- Mockplus (for designing, prototyping, and handoff)

Tools for Accounting and Managing Invoices

These tools are used for accounting purposes such as managing invoices, recording expenses, and other financial-related input that can help your agency store essential information.

- Zoho Books
- Quickbooks
- Xero
- FreshBooks
- Sage
- Wave

Key Takeaways From This Chapter

- You can scale your agency by utilizing any of these four scaling strategies or models: the default sales funnel, the outsourcing model, the webinar model, or the SaaS subscription model.
- You can scale an agency by laying foundations early on and building a team that fits your agency's core values and culture, building a team of leaders, celebrating each milestone, and adapting at every turn.
- You can also scale your business faster financially by saying no to clients who let you down, working with clients who have bigger budgets, and being strict with getting paid on time.
- Map out an organizational structure and hire candidates by expanding outreach, making succession plans, researching skills required, and improving your agency's reputation.
- Utilize digital tools to help your team improve their workflow and automate basic processes. This helps you to deliver results consistently and scale your business faster.

Conclusion

Realize what you really want. It stops you from chasing butterflies and puts you to work digging gold.

— William Moulton Marston

We have reached the end of the book, and we have covered the fundamentals of starting your digital marketing agency from scratch and becoming successful at it.

In this book, we have covered the following:

- the digital marketing concepts
- the importance of setting and measuring digital marketing goals
- targeting the right type of clients for your digital marketing business as per your client acquisition process
- list of digital marketing services that you can sell and the importance of focusing on a niche

- the importance of using digital tools for your business and for clients to keep thriving
- ways to retain and keep building a bigger client base
- ways to scale and automate your digital marketing agency to better efficiency and growth

I hope you can take these lessons and apply them diligently in real-world situations as you run your digital marketing agency.

Don't doubt yourself for a moment. If you are passionate about digital marketing, it won't be a mistake, and personally, I've found so much joy as a proud owner of an agency that has become successful and fulfilling in my life. I wish the same for you.

If you have enjoyed the lessons in this book, kindly share your thoughts and leave a review. Till then, I wish you the best with your digital marketing agency.

Thank You

I want to give a big thank you to everyone who has bought my book. I hope you enjoyed the book and found it helpful.

If you could please take a moment to write a review on the platform, it would mean a lot to me. Your reviews help other people find my work and enjoy it, too. It will also help me write the kind of books that will help you get the results you want in your business.

Thanks again for taking the time to read my work and I hope to hear from you soon!

>> Leave a review on Amazon US <<
>> Leave a review on Amazon UK <<

References

5 Effective Talent Acquisition Strategies that will Help Hiring Managers Scale their Teams in Half the Time. (n.d.). Recruiter. https://www.recruiter.com/recruiting/5-effective-talent-acquisition-strategies-that-will-help-hiring-managers-scale-their-teams-in-half-the-time/

6 Reasons to Start a Digital Marketing Agency. (2019, April 1). Digital Deepak ®. https://digitaldeepak.com/start-a-digital-marketing-agency/

7-Step Sales Process: When to Use It and When to Break It. (2017, October 12). Lucidchart.com. https://www.lucidchart.com/blog/what-is-the-7-step-sales-process

7 tips to create an effective digital marketing budget. (n.d.). Spendesk. https://www.spendesk.com/en-eu/blog/digital-marketing-budget/

8 Benefits of Digital Marketing: All You Should Know. (2021, June 29). Simplilearn. https://www.simplilearn.com/digital-marketing-benefits-article

10 KPIs to monitor your digital marketing performance. (n.d.). www.klipfolio.com. https://www.klipfolio.com/blog/marketing-kpis-to-measure-digital-marketing-performance

11 Actionable Ways to Build Client Relationships That Last. (n.d.). WordStream. https://www.wordstream.com/blog/ws/2021/06/21/build-client-relationships

20 Digital Marketing Resources Every Business Needs in Their Arsenal. (n.d.). Www.bluleadz.com. https://www.bluleadz.com/blog/15-places-to-get-the-best-digital-marketing-resources

43 Marketing Agency Tools to Help You Scale. (n.d.). AgencyAnalytics. https://agencyanalytics.com/blog/marketing-agency-tools

Carmicheal, K. (2022, April 12). *Is A Media Mix Right for Your Brand?* Blog.hubspot.com. https://blog.hubspot.com/marketing/media-mix

Cezim, B. (2023, January 11). *Choosing a Niche for Your Digital Agency: Industries to Focus On in 2023.* Digital Agency Network. https://digitalagencynetwork.com/choosing-a-niche-for-your-digital-agency-which-industries-to-focus-on/

Chaffey, D. (2020, October 5). *Setting Goals for Your Digital Marketing | Smart Insights.* Smart Insights. https://www.smartinsights.com/goal-setting-evaluation/goals-kpis/goals-for-your-digital-marketing/

CIM. (2022, September 1). *Five stages of your customers' buying journey |*

References

CIM Exchange. Www.cim.co.uk. https://www.cim.co.uk/content-hub/blog/five-stages-of-your-customers-buying-journey/

Conley, M. (2019). *How to Manage Your Entire Marketing Budget [Free Budget Planner Templates].* Hubspot.com. https://blog.hubspot.com/marketing/how-to-manage-marketing-budget-free-budget-templates

Create a Marketing Plan For Social Media in 8 Steps. (n.d.). Mailchimp. https://mailchimp.com/resources/marketing-plan-for-social-media/

Digital Marketing Agency Tools: Top 18 Tools for 2023. (n.d.). Whatagraph. https://whatagraph.com/blog/articles/best-digital-marketing-agency-tools

Digital Marketing Metrics: 14 to Keep an Eye on in 2021. (2021, January 28). Rock Content. https://rockcontent.com/blog/digital-marketing-metrics/

Digital Marketing Team Structure. (2021, June 4). Equinet Academy. https://www.equinetacademy.com/digital-marketing-team-structure/

Dublino, J. (2022, June 29). *10 Tips for Building an Effective Business Website.* Www.businessnewsdaily.com. https://www.businessnewsdaily.com/9811-effective-business-website-tips.html

Forsey, C. (2016). T*he Ultimate Guide to Relationship Marketing.* Hubspot.com. https://blog.hubspot.com/marketing/relationship-marketing

How to create a digital marketing budget? | Outbrain.com. (2019, December 11). English (US). https://www.outbrain.com/blog/marketing-budget-planning/

How To Get Clients For Digital Marketing In 2021. (n.d.). Snovio Labs. https://snov.io/blog/how-to-get-clients-for-digital-marketing/

How to Get Clients for Your Digital Marketing Agency in 2021. (2020, December 9). Digital Agency Network. https://digitalagencynetwork.com/how-to-get-clients-for-your-digital-marketing-agency/

How to Get More Clients for Your Digital Marketing Agency. (n.d.). Metrics Watch. https://metricswatch.com/how-to-get-more-clients-for-your-digital-marketing-agency

How to Write a Follow-Up Email (+12 Examples & Templates). (n.d.). WordStream. https://www.wordstream.com/blog/ws/2022/05/09/follow-up-email

How to write a sales email: 6 sales email examples that work. (n.d.). Zendesk. https://www.zendesk.com/in/blog/sales-email-examples/

Key Concepts In Digital Marketing Guide – Skills Gap Trainer. (n.d.). https://skillsgaptrainer.com/key-concepts-in-digital-marketing/

Magaline, V. (2020, May 18). *17 Must-Have Digital Marketing Agency*

Tools in 2023. Customers.ai. https://customers.ai/blog/marketing-agency-tools

Moon, K. (n.d.). *Example of a Full Digital Marketing Plan and Budget.* Ascend Business Growth. https://www.ascendbusinessgrowth.com/blog/example-of-monthly-inbound-marketing-plan

Varikkodan, A. (2022, April 8). *What are the 7 Ps of marketing?* Online Manipal. https://www.onlinemanipal.com/blogs/what-are-the-seven-ps-of-marketing

What Are Digital Marketing Goals and Objectives? | Wrike Guide. (n.d.). Www.wrike.com. https://www.wrike.com/digital-marketing-guide/faq/what-are-digital-marketing-goals-objectives/

What Are Productized Services? (2021, March 1). Neil Patel. https://neilpatel.com/blog/productized-services/

What Is a Landing Page? Landing Pages Explained | Unbounce. (2010). Unbounce. https://unbounce.com/landing-page-articles/what-is-a-landing-page/

What is a media mix and why is it important? (n.d.). Amazon Advertising Blog. https://advertising.amazon.com/blog/media-mix

What Is a Value Ladder? Definition & Examples. (n.d.). Mighty Networks. https://www.mightynetworks.com/encyclopedia/value-ladder

What is CLV? Why Customer Lifetime Value Matters - Mailchimp. (n.d.). Mailchimp. https://mailchimp.com/clv/

What is Customer Lifetime Value (CLV) | Definition, Formula & Calculation. (2021, October 1). Essential Business Guides. https://www.zoho.com/subscriptions/guides/what-is-customer-lifetime-value-clv.html

What is customer retention? (n.d.). Salesforce.com. https://www.salesforce.com/eu/learning-centre/customer-service/customer-retention/

What is Performance Marketing? [Definition & Examples]. (n.d.). Careerfoundry.com. https://careerfoundry.com/en/blog/digital-marketing/performance-marketing/

What Services Do Digital Marketing Agencies Offer? (n.d.). Semrush Blog. https://www.semrush.com/blog/digital-marketing-agency-services-list/

White, R. (2019). *27 Ways to Drive Traffic to Your Website.* Hubspot.com. https://blog.hubspot.com/marketing/increase-website-traffic

WordStream. (2023). *Social Media Marketing for Businesses | WordStream.* Wordstream. https://www.wordstream.com/social-media-marketing

The anatomy of a landing page: 9 essential elements with examples. (2022, December 16). Wix Blog. https://www.wix.com/blog/2022/12/anatomy-of-a-landing-page/

149

www.ingramcontent.com/pod-product-compliance
Lightning Source LLC
Chambersburg PA
CBHW030521210326
41597CB00013B/979